THE OFFICIAL NBA FINALS 2001 RETROSPECTIVE

CLOSE TWO A DYNASTY

BY LYLE SPENCER

PUBLISHED BY

The SportingNews

PHOTOGRAPHY BY NBA ENTERTAINMENT PHOTOS

DESIGNED AND PRODUCED BY RARE AIR MEDIA

CREDITS

Designed and Produced by: Rare Air Media
1711 N. Paulina, Suite 311, Chicago, Ill. 60622

Published by: Vulcan Sports Media, DBA The Sporting News
10176 Corporate Square Drive, Suite 200, St. Louis, Mo. 63132

The SportingNews

Library of Congress Cataloging-in-Publication Data is available from the Publisher.

ISBN 0-89204-667-8

Printed in the United States of America.

9 8 7 6 5 4 3 2

First Edition

ACKNOWLEDGEMENTS

To put together a book such as this, on the fly with deadlines coming faster than a Sixers double team, you need a total effort not unlike the two-time champion Lakers have used to rule their world. In our eclectic troupe, I think of chief editor Jan Hubbard as the Zen master, coolly making all the right moves. In the role of Shaq, a towering presence with a rare combination of warmth and intelligent wit, is the wondrous Jeanne Tang. The superb photographers are the "Super Friends," as Rick Fox dubbed the role players in Shaq's orbit. Finally, let me flatter myself as the Kobe of this project, trying to merge my efforts with my formidable teammates and turn that clutch phrase when it matters most, at winnin' time.

This, personally, is for the three legends who made a Santa Monica kid's heart sing. I wore No. 22 one year in high school for Elgin Baylor; No. 44 the next, for Jerry West, Mr. Clutch. It was a thrill pulling on those jerseys, even if I was a pale imitation of the originals. The breathless voice bringing it to life, the triumphs and too frequent postseason despairs, belonged to Chick Hearn, simply the greatest ever to put mustard on a hotdog and yo-yo his way through the most compelling broadcasts in the history of man.

Championship No. 8 in Los Angeles takes its special place. It seemed fitting that this team resembled in so many respects the first Lakers champions of 1971-72, the Sharman / Wilt / West / Goodrich juggernaut that won 33 in a dazzling row. I was a pup reporter then; a decade later I would cover the greatest teams I've seen, the "Showtime" Lakers of Buck, Big Fella, Big Game James, Silk, Slick Norm, Coop, Doo, Firin' Byron, Blue Collar Kurt and the rest. I've been blessed to get to know these remarkable people. To Elegant Elgin, Zeke from Cabin Creek and Chickie Baby, three giants who laid the foundation 40 years ago, no tribute is sufficient. A simple thanks will have to do.

Lyle Spencer — June 2001

SPECIAL THANKS

At NBA Editorial:
John Hareas, Barry Rubinstein, John Gardella, Rob Reheuser, Chris Ekstrand, April Bulger and Matthew Wesley

At Rare Air Media:
Mark Vancil, Frank Fochetta, John Vieceli, Andy Pipitone, Dennis Carlson, Melinda Fry, Shannon Mounts,
Nick LoBue, Nick DeCarlo and Steve Polacek

At the NBA:
David Stern, Russ Granik, Brian McIntyre, Terry Lyons

At NBA Entertainment Photos:
Carmin Romanelli, Joe Amati, Jesse Garrabrant, David Bonilla, Pam Healy, Michael Klein, Scott Yurdin,
John Kristofick, Bennett Renda and Chris Chambers

At NBA Entertainment:
Adam Silver, Gregg Winik, Heidi Ueberroth, Charles Rosenzweig, Paul Hirschheimer, Marc Hirschheimer,
Michael Levine, Meredith Tanchum and David Mory

At The Sporting News:
Marilyn Kasal, Kathy Kinkeade, Steve Meyerhoff, David Walton

Also:
Phil Jackson, Jim Perzik, John Black, Tim Harris, Michael Uhlenkamp, Alison Bogli and the entire Lakers organization,
Larry Brown, Dave Coskey, Karen Frascona, Harvey Pollack, Brian Kirschner, Chris Wallace and the entire Sixers organization,
Jordan Brenner and John Fawaz

CONTENTS

PARADE OF CHAMPIONS DAY

1

A BEAMING SHAQUILLE O'NEAL ROARED INTO STAPLES CENTER IN THE MORNING SUNLIGHT ON HIS CUSTOM-MADE HARLEY-DAVIDSON. A BLACK LEATHER VEST THAT WAS INSCRIBED WITH "SHAQ" WAS ADORNING HIS MASSIVE FRAME — AS IF HE WOULDN'T BE INSTANTLY IDENTIFIED BY EVERY LIVING SOUL IN LOS ANGELES. IT WAS PARADE OF CHAMPIONS DAY, THREE DAYS AFTER THE LAKERS HAD WON THEIR SECOND CONSECUTIVE TITLE, AND THE HOMETOWN CORONATION WAS AT HAND.

Moments later, an expression-less Kobe Bryant parked his Mercedes and strolled inside the arena, clutching the gold NBA Championship trophy, his bride of two months Vanessa Laine at his side. There would be thousands of gold No. 8 jerseys visible on this day of celebration, but Kobe wasn't

inside one of them. An authentic Lakers jersey from another era — No. 44 — had replaced his No. 8.
"You can't buy these," Kobe said. "Jerry West gave it to me. I'm wearing it in his honor."
Bryant, in fact, attempted to purchase a replica West jersey on Father's Day, but couldn't find

one. So he solved the problem in a conversation with West. "I had to call him up and ask for one," Bryant said.

Shaq and Kobe were, as always, a study in contrasts, men entirely different in all respects except one. They shared a burning desire to win championships. After an irregular season of false starts, wrong turns and hurtful words, they finally discovered that they were more alike than different; competitive all the same, but still very much bonded by their lust for titles. When that revelation struck both, the Lakers became stable, domineering and, to the rest of the league, frightening. Blessed with the NBA's most powerful player and most refined player, how could they possibly lose?

They didn't . . . except once. An inspired 107-101 overtime triumph by the Philadelphia 76ers in Game 1 of the Finals was the only blemish on a 15-1 playoff record, the best in NBA history. The Lakers also ended the regular season with eight consecutive victories, giving them 23 wins in the final 24 games they played in the 2000-01 NBA season.

Close to a dynasty? After winning their second consecutive title, there is little to suggest otherwise. Shaq is 29; Kobe is 22. Surround them with a group of effective role players, and the bar is set incredibly high.

"Can . . . you . . . dig it?" Shaq shouted during a celebration bringing an estimated 550,000 fans to downtown Los Angeles for what became, at the Big Rapper's insistence, the biggest party ever staged in a city notorious for its laid-back attitude — in all things not related to basketball.

Oh, yes, they dug it. Along the 12-block Figueroa Street parade route, kids in oversize Lakers jerseys from the barrio mingled with briefcase-toting executives in three-piece suits, everyone bonded by the love of a team that has unified a city for four decades. Lakermania reached epic proportions during the title repeat, momentum gathering as the team rolled through the Western Conference playoffs unbeaten, knocking off powerhouses Portland, Sacramento and San Antonio with astonishing grace and ease. The 76ers offered unexpected resistance before they, too, were run over by Phil Jackson's state-of-the-art steamroller.

"Wouldn't it be sweet to repeat?" Jackson asked the throng that had gathered after the parade in a parking lot outside STAPLES Center to

catch one last glimpse of their heroes on stage.

Magic Johnson, part owner and orchestrator of five titles in the "Showtime" era, took the microphone and labeled the 2000-2001 champs "the greatest team that's ever played. We salute you and honor you."

The Lakers praised their followers — "my friends," Shaq called them — for their inspirational support.

"We told ya'll last year we were going to do it again," Bryant said, spraying a huge squirt gun. "We did it again! We're going back to get another one next year. Back to back to back!" To show what he meant, Kobe stood back to back to back with Brian Shaw and Tyronn Lue, who wore a Shaq jersey that fell almost to the ground.

The big finale could mean only one thing: Diesel time. Out came the man himself, posing like a bodybuilder. Shaq's people loved it.

They laughed. They chanted and cheered. They rocked and swayed, locking arms and bouncing off one another just as the Lakers were doing behind their leader as he pranced across the stage.

"Three-peat!" Shaq shouted into the microphone.

"Three-peat!" chanted back his friends of all sizes, shapes, genders and nationalities. O'Neal took over the celebration with the force of his personality in the same way that he

had seized control of the Finals with the power of his unconquerable game.

"The most dominating player in the history of the NBA," legendary play-by-play voice Chick Hearn had said while introducing O'Neal, and who was to argue with Chickie Baby now?

Four-time NBA Defensive Player of the Year Dikembe Mutombo played with all the knowledge and ferocity he could summon, but

O'Neal came out roaring and never stopped on his way to back-to-back Finals MVP awards, something previously achieved only by Michael Jordan and Hakeem Olajuwon. "The guy is a monster, man," a beaten Mutombo said.

O'Neal averaged 30.4 points, 15.4 rebounds, 3.2 assists and 2.4 blocks in 16 postseason games.

Bryant was a dream complement to O'Neal, running the offense with a cool precision belying his 22 years

while averaging 29.4 points, 7.3 rebounds, 6.1 assists and 1.6 steals.

League MVP Allen Iverson, whose 48 points had carried the 76ers to that stunning Game 1 victory, went down firing. But Larry Brown's depleted Sixers, battered and beaten down by seven-game series with Toronto and Milwaukee, finally surrendered to a Lakers outfit that was evoking comparisons with the greatest teams in NBA history.

While those debates would rage on into next season, no one could dispute that the Lakers' superior postseason run (15-1), surpassing the 12-1 standard set by Philadelphia's 1982-83 champs.

"With Shaq and Kobe at the age they are," Lakers power forward Horace Grant said, "I give it eight, nine more titles."

West, having turned personnel duties over to Mitch Kupchak after the 1999-2000 season, built the

team primarily in the summer of 1996 when he acquired Bryant in a trade with Charlotte involving Vlade Divac, drafted unheralded Derek Fisher out of Arkansas-Little Rock and completed the trifecta by landing O'Neal as a free agent.

"When basketball is played correctly with good players," West said, "it is something great to see. It looks easy, but it's not. That's a tribute not only to the players, but also to Phil Jackson and his staff, who got the

players to buy into what they wanted. That's Phil's plan, having all the players touch the ball and watching everyone contribute. That's how basketball should be played."

The two superstars paid homage to West, saying that he was the influence that guided them, making them practice what he preached.

"Mr. West promised me he would always keep a great team around me — and he kept his promise," O'Neal said.

"Jerry's the man who got me and Shaq and Fish here," Bryant said, explaining why he wore West's jersey to the parade. "He's the reason we're all here today. With everything that went on this season, he meant so much to me."

All that was left were those confident promises of a three-peat.

"The only team that can beat us," Shaq said, "is us."

Twenty-eight other franchises fear that he is right.

SHAQ & KOBE: MAKING IT WORK

2

THE DEFINING MOMENT IN THE LOS ANGELES LAKERS' 2000-01 TITLE RUN DIDN'T COME ON THE COURT, INSTEAD RESONATING OUT OF VIEW OF FANS AND CAMERA CREWS. SHAQUILLE O'NEAL STOPPED BY KOBE BRYANT'S LOCKER IN A CORNER OF THE VISITORS' DRESSING ROOM AT SAN ANTONIO'S ALAMODOME, EXTENDED THE KNUCKLES OF HIS RIGHT FIST TO MEET BRYANT'S, AND SAID: "YOU'RE MY IDOL, BRO."

A few months earlier, Shaq and Kobe going fist to fist would have had a different meaning entirely, with dire consequences.

A long and sometimes draining season, loaded with bitter words, posturing and vague threats of ending the relationship from both camps, distilled to this one quiet moment of reconciliation in the afterglow of Game 1 of the Western Conference Finals. The Combo was back, more formidable than ever. The Twin Towers, soon to be swept into next season, were no match for the Twin Powers in the Lakers' 2001 Space Odyssey.

"It caught me off guard," Kobe said, describing his initial reaction to O'Neal's stunning endorsement.

Shaq didn't stop there. He told teammates he wanted to name a son Sha-Kobe, after Bryant.

"I said, 'Don't do that to that kid,'" Bryant said, grinning.

Striding to the podium for the postgame press conference O'Neal said of Bryant, who had rocked the Spurs' foundation with 45 points in a 104-90 decision: "I told Kobe he's my idol." When laughter filled the room, Shaq dropped his head slightly and plunged forward.

"No, I'm serious. He's phenomenal. He's the best player in the league, by far, when he's playing like that — scoring, getting everybody involved, playing good defense. That's where I've been trying to get him all year. I can now say he's the best player. He's the best on all nine planets."

O'Neal, of course, can afford to be extravagant in his praise of Kobe

SHAQ AND KOBE

because Shaq's no slouch on the basketball court himself.

"Shaq obviously is the most dominant player in the league," said Bryant, the other member of the mutual admiration society. "What

people fail to realize is how much he's grown mentally. Calls that might have gotten him down in the past, now he plays right through it, bulls right through it."

Bryant and his teammates were

delighted to see O'Neal perform like No. 34 of old — the 2000 league and Finals MVP — as the 2001 postseason moved along. Shaq slam-dunked Portland in a three-game sweep, then rocked Sacramento in two

games for 87 points and 41 rebounds with unprecedented back-to-back 40-20 performances in the West semifinals. In the three sweeps before the Finals, O'Neal averaged 29.3 points and 15.3 rebounds.

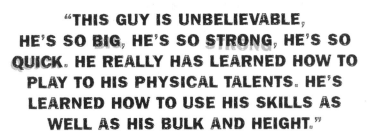

"THIS GUY IS UNBELIEVABLE, HE'S SO BIG, HE'S SO STRONG, HE'S SO QUICK. HE REALLY HAS LEARNED HOW TO PLAY TO HIS PHYSICAL TALENTS. HE'S LEARNED HOW TO USE HIS SKILLS AS WELL AS HIS BULK AND HEIGHT."

— RICK ADELMAN —

"This guy is unbelievable," said Sacramento skipper Rick Adelman. "He's so big, he's so strong, he's so quick. He really has learned how to play to his physical talents. He's learned how to use his skills as well as his bulk and height."

Shaq agreed.

"I know how to position and contort myself, and because of the big ass I possess, I'm able to get position," he said. "I don't shoot jump shots, fadeaways. It's not that

I'm a great shooter, I'm making the shots I take."

That was not always the case this season. O'Neal, judged by his own lofty standards, started the season off key. The feud with Bryant didn't help matters as Shaq and the Lakers settled into the middle of the pack in the Western Conference. But after an April 1 loss to New York at home, the Lakers began their amazing surge with O'Neal back in prime physical condition.

In the eight-game winning streak leading into the postseason, O'Neal averaged 34 points and 12.8 rebounds. The Big Repeat run was underway, and the sniping between the superstars ceased.

"Winning obviously brings up the spirits of everybody on the team," Bryant said. "I think that brings us closer together. We're cool."

"As a staff," veteran assistant coach Tex Winter said, "we thought it was overblown. I don't think there's any question there was resentment, with Shaq particularly. But we didn't think it was anything that couldn't be worked out. Coach Jackson is a master of team management. It's his great strength. He sees things in their total perspective.

"Super players have super egos. They wouldn't be here if they didn't. They take challenges, sometimes with a teammate. It's the nature of the beast."

"SUPER PLAYERS HAVE SUPER EGOS. THEY WOULDN'T BE HERE IF THEY DIDN'T. THEY TAKE CHALLENGES, SOMETIMES WITH A TEAMMATE. IT'S THE NATURE OF THE BEAST."

— TEX WINTER —

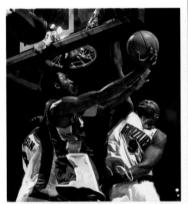

In the face of mounting media pressure, Jackson resisted bringing the two stars together in a sit-down during their cold war.

"P.J. has great patience," assistant coach Jim Cleamons said.

Sure enough, there he was, grinning knowingly as he watched Shaq and Kobe praise each other and make sweet music again when it counted. Jackson had his eighth ring as a head coach in the NBA.

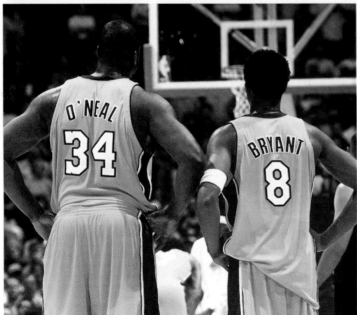

PHIL AND THE ROLE PLAYERS

IN THE MIND OF LEGENDARY COLLEGE COACH JOHN WOODEN, PHIL JACKSON'S MOST PRESSING CHALLENGE IN HIS QUEST FOR THE LAKERS TO REPEAT AS CHAMPIONS WAS NOT IN FINDING HARMONIOUS MIDDLE GROUND FOR SHAQUILLE O'NEAL AND KOBE BRYANT. THAT, UCLA'S 10-TIME NATIONAL CHAMPION SUGGESTED, WAS OVERRATED.

"I don't think his biggest job was with Kobe and Shaq," Wooden said. "It was in getting the other fellows to accept their roles."

That happens to be one of Jackson's strengths. A role-playing backup forward on Red Holzman's finely tuned New York Knicks teams of the late '60s and early '70s, Jackson has a keen awareness of the needs and desires of the lesser lights surrounding the stars.

"It's esprit de corps," Jackson said. "It's that element that makes basketball such a great community game."

Most of Jackson's philosophies were shaped by Holzman, Willis Reed, his buddy Bill Bradley and the rest of the Knicks.

"I want the players to understand they're the first and most primary reason we're winning," Jackson said. "The guys that are on the court are what counts. If they don't have a

way to get along together, no matter what we do strategically — all the preparation we do, you can be the greatest X and O guy in the world — nothing works. It's all on them."

Zen and the art of basketball maintenance is a fulltime job.

"His background as a role player obviously is a big help to Phil in terms of relating to the support players now," said Bill Bertka, the Lakers' longtime assistant coach

and former scout. "His big concern is that they play good, solid basketball within the system. Support players flourish in his style of coaching. You saw it in Chicago with the Bulls, and you're seeing it now with the Lakers. But it has to be a particular type of support player, one who's able to play within his system, read defenses, play defense, and work within the team framework."

HORACE GRANT

ROBERT HORRY

DEREK FISHER

RICK FOX

BRIAN SHAW

PHIL JACKSON

"I WANT THE PLAYERS TO UNDERSTAND THEY'RE THE FIRST AND MOST PRIMARY REASON WE'RE WINNING. THE GUYS THAT ARE ON THE COURT ARE WHAT COUNTS. IF THEY DON'T HAVE A WAY TO GET ALONG TOGETHER, NO MATTER WHAT WE DO STRATEGICALLY — ALL THE PREPARATION WE DO, YOU CAN BE THE GREATEST X AND O GUY IN THE WORLD — NOTHING WORKS. IT'S ALL ON THEM."

— PHIL JACKSON —

ROBERT HORRY

BRIAN SHAW

RICK FOX

HORACE GRANT

DEREK FISHER

SUPERSUBS ROBERT HORRY AND BRIAN SHAW WOULD BE GETTING MOST OF THE MINUTES BEHIND STARTERS O'NEAL, BRYANT, RICK FOX, HORACE GRANT AND DEREK FISHER. RON HARPER AND YOUNG PROS TYRONN LUE, MARK MADSEN AND DEVEAN GEORGE WOULD BE SUMMONED FOR OCCASIONAL RELIEF.

RON HARPER

TYRONN LUE

MARK MADSEN

DEVEAN GEORGE

Roles shifted over the course of the long regular season. Jackson even found a role for CBA journeyman Mike Penberthy, who provided offense for a time in the injury-riddled backcourt. But in April, the Lakers kicked into high gear and Jackson had perfected his rotation. He would go essentially with seven men, rather than the deeper rotation deployed in the 2000 playoff run. Supersubs Robert Horry and Brian Shaw would be getting most of the minutes behind starters O'Neal, Bryant, Rick Fox, Horace Grant and Derek Fisher. Ron Harper and young pros Tyronn Lue, Mark Madsen and Devean George would be summoned for occasional relief.

Cast in a reduced role because of a midseason knee injury was one of Jackson's favorites, Harper, the veteran guard who was on three of Jackson's championship teams in Chicago. A starter last season and up to Feb. 13 this year, Harper moved aside when Fisher, the fifth-year point guard from Arkansas- Little Rock, returned from a stress fracture to his right foot.

Fisher had a big night in his debut, hitting 8 of 16 shots for 26 points against Boston on March 13. He did not leave the starting lineup, serving as a catalyst for a 15-5 finish that sent the Lakers surging into the postseason with an eight-game winning streak.

"Derek isn't a role player anymore — he's a star," Bertka said after the lefty hit 11 of 13 shots, including 6 of 7 from three-point range, for a career-high 28 points in the 111-82 Game 4 victory that swept San Antonio in the Western Conference Finals.

In the four games against the Spurs, Fisher had an NBA record 15 threes, shooting 75 percent from beyond the arc while averaging 17.5 points. This from a man who'd averaged 4.7 points and shot 43 percent as a fourth guard in the 2000 postseason, and who had undergone surgery.

"DEREK ISN'T A ROLE PLAYER ANYMORE – HE'S A STAR." — BILL BERTKA, LAKERS ASSISTANT

"It was a very serious injury, one that has caused careers to end," Fisher said. "Before the injury, I thought too much about what other people thought of me. Now I just play. I take the responsibility of providing spark for our team — not necessarily offensively, but taking charges, going to the floor, hitting the open man and playing solid defense. The trust I got from my teammates was a big factor."

All through the postseason, the defensive efforts of Fox, Grant and Horry up front with the shot-altering O'Neal were central to the Lakers' success. Such formidable threats as Scottie Pippen, Rasheed Wallace, Chris Webber, Peja Stojakovic and Tim Duncan were frustrated repeatedly by the three veteran forwards.

Fox, who turned 32 in July, is the quintessential role player, on and off the court. He has had a recurring role in the HBO series *Oz* as a character who makes the NBA's toughest

hombres look like choirboys. He also lost 25 pounds in the offseason, which his coaches credit as a major reason for his success this year.

"Players with great talent are going to play a lot of good games," Jackson said. "He put together numbers of good games, and that's important. With players that we would call our complementary players, we need guys like Rick to step up and give us 15, 20 points, because teams are going to be helping out so much on Kobe and Shaq that we've got to have that complementary package."

Fox moved into the starting small forward slot when Glen Rice was dealt to New York in a blockbuster deal that made a Laker of the 35-year-old Grant.

Not many teams are asked to defend a title with three new starters, but Fox, Grant and Fisher all were familiar with the triangle offense. Grant won three titles as a Chicago Bull under Jackson in the early '90s, and Fox and Fisher were

"... WE NEED GUYS LIKE RICK TO STEP UP AND GIVE US 15, 20 POINTS ..." — PHIL JACKSON

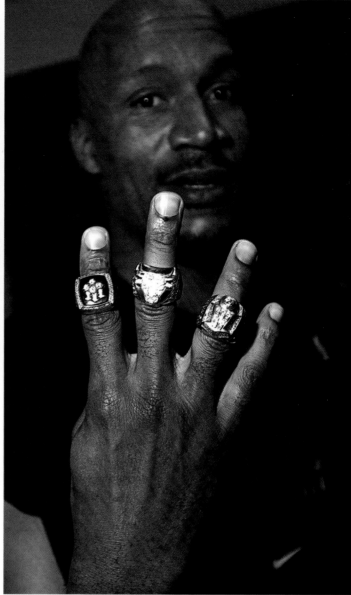

ready reserves during the Lakers' 2000 title run.

Grant was no stranger to Jackson or O'Neal, his former teammate in Orlando, when he arrived in L.A. from Seattle in the four-team swap that sent Rice to New York and Patrick Ewing to the Sonics.

"We needed defense," Jackson said. "We got hurt last year a lot at that position. That's a great position out here in the West. We needed someone athletic and defensive and strong enough that we can take care of that."

Grant humbly accepted the assignment. "This day and age," he said, "no one guy is going to stop one guy, regardless. It's going to be a team effort. I do the best I can."

At 6-10, with remarkable speed, quickness and anticipation, Horry is able to defend a variety of players while running the floor for dunks and drilling three-pointers. He showed his clutch nature as a starting forward for Houston's two-time champions (1994 and 95) and again as a force off the bench with the Lakers' 2000 titlists.

"I've always been a warm-weather player," Horry said, **explaining why he does his best work at playoff time. "When the weather heats up, so do I. I've always enjoyed playing in big games. It's what brings out the best in an athlete."**

When Shaw, a 6-6 guard who'd played for six NBA clubs, found his way to L.A. after a 1999 season he teamed with O'Neal, an old buddy from Orlando, in what came to be known as the "Shaw-Shaq Redemption." Shaw, in his ninth trip to the postseason, brought intelligence, defense, an outside threat and a matchless knack for throwing the lob to Shaq and Kobe.

Harper, once one of the game's most gifted athletes, is the classic example of the player who aged gracefully and does as much with his personality as his tools.

"Let me tell you," Harper said, **"if I wasn't playing for Phil, I would have said bye-bye by now. Because Phil is a guy who knows what needs to be done. He's a guy who has his hands on the game. It's a fun job playing for him."**

For Harper, who made it clear this was his last go-round, the ring's the thing.

"You can never have too many of them," he said, grinning. "Never."

"LET ME TELL YOU, IF I WASN'T PLAYING FOR PHIL, I WOULD HAVE SAID BYE-BYE BY NOW. BECAUSE PHIL IS A GUY WHO KNOWS WHAT NEEDS TO BE DONE. HE'S A GUY WHO HAS HIS HANDS ON THE GAME. IT'S A FUN JOB PLAYING FOR HIM."

— RON HARPER —

SEASON IN REVIEW

GAME 75 OF THE LAKERS "UNDERACHIEVING" SEASON WAS TO BE LITTLE MORE THAN A PIT STOP IN UTAH. WHILE THEIR 48-26 RECORD WAS GOOD ENOUGH FOR SECOND PLACE IN THE PACIFIC DIVISION, IT WAS ALSO 14 GAMES OFF THE PACE THEY HAD SET THE PREVIOUS SEASON. FACTOR IN THE REAL OR EMBELLISHED — DEPENDING ON WHO WAS TELLING THE STORY — SHAQUILLE O'NEAL-KOBE BRYANT FEUD, AND THE LAKERS SEEMED TO BE SENDING A VERY CLEAR MESSAGE THAT THEY WERE GOING TO END THEIR OWN DYNASTY AFTER ONLY ONE YEAR.

The longest winning streak the Lakers had built during the regular season was five games. Even if they won their final eight games — unlikely considering the next four were on the road — they would still finish the season 11 games worse than 1999-2000 when they were 67-15. At a time when the basketball world was scratching its collective head and wondering how the wondrously talented team could have blown it so badly, the slumbering giant awoke. The remainder of the season was nothing less than perfect:

April 3 at Utah: 96-88
April 5 at Chicago: 100-88
April 6 at Boston: 100-96
April 8 at Minnesota: 104-99

And those four games were without Bryant, who had missed nine of the previous 10 games since spraining his left ankle. O'Neal, however, had Bryant's back, averaging 35.8 points and 11.5 rebounds in those games while shooting 60.3 percent from the free throw line.

"THERE'S NO WAY TO GUARD ME, NOBODY IN THIS LEAGUE IS QUICK ENOUGH TO TAKE AWAY EVERY MOVE I HAVE."

— SHAQUILLE O'NEAL —

> **"IF HE'S [BRYANT] ABLE TO BLEND HIS TALENT AND SLIDE BACK IN SEAMLESSLY, HE CAN ADJUST IN TWO OR THREE GAMES, OTHERWISE, IF OUR OFFENSE HAS TO STOP TO GET READJUSTED AS HE GETS BACK IN, IT'LL BE A LITTLE LONGER."**
>
> — PHIL JACKSON —

"There's no way to guard me," said a confident O'Neal. **"Nobody in this league is quick enough to take away every move I have."**

With four games left, Bryant returned. The Lakers would be stronger, yet Jackson was a little concerned about losing momentum.

"If he's able to blend his talent and slide back in seamlessly, he can adjust in two or three games," Lakers coach Phil Jackson said. "Otherwise, if our offense has to stop to get readjusted as he gets back in, it'll be a little longer."

Bryant provided the answer emphatically in L.A.'s next game against Phoenix and proved Jackson wrong by a game or two, sliding seamlessly into the Lakers' flow. **With a healthy Bryant back, L.A. kept rolling:** Sharing the workload, O'Neal and Bryant combined to score 53 percent of their team's remaining points as the Lakers averaged 109.5 points over the final four regular-season games:

April 10 vs. Phoenix: 106-80
April 12 vs. Minnesota: 119-102
April 15 vs. Portland: 105-100

April 17 vs. Denver: 108-91
The Lakers were obviously optimistic.

"If we can develop some consistency and keep playing this way," O'Neal said, "we have a better shot of doing what we did last season."

Suddenly, the Lakers, who were maligned for most of the season, were the hottest team entering the

playoffs. Their late spurt enabled them to sneak past the potent Sacramento Kings to capture the division title and the No. 2 seed in the Western Conference. O'Neal and Bryant were the league's best inside-outside duo. The role players were perfect in their roles. And, perhaps most importantly, the team was playing stifling defense.

"We feel fortunate we had the opportunity to come into this position where we have home court, finish second in the conference, first in our division," Jackson said. **"The responsibility was up to us to do it at the end of the season."**

Lost in the early-season Shaq-Kobe power struggle that was well documented throughout the league, were two important points:

- Three-fifths of the Lakers' starting lineup was new with Rick Fox at small forward, Horace Grant at power forward and Derek Fisher at the point.
- Injuries had limited the Lakers all season. Fisher, Bryant, O'Neal and Ron Harper had all spent time convalescing.

Fox raised his scoring average to 12.1 points after the All-Star break, up from 7.7 points in the first half of the season. Grant provided blue-collar defense against the Chris Webbers and Tim Duncans of the basketball universe. Robert Horry, Brian Shaw and Harper provided defense and perimeter shooting. And Fisher? Well, once the diminutive 6-1, 200-pound guard re-entered the Lakers' rotation March 13 after missing the first 62 games of the season with a stress fracture injury to his right foot, the Lakers went 15-5.

"He's a great player; a point guard that's going to bring it all together," said Kings center Vlade Divac. "Especially taking the pressure from Shaq and Kobe, because everybody knows they're the Lakers' two main guys. So, if you add Derek Fisher, they are still the champions."

Eventually, the key players regained their health, rededicated themselves to the greater good of the team, and set their sights on defending their title.

Finally, that goal seemed within reach.

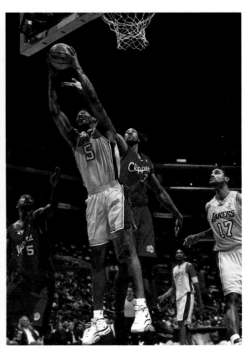

THE
PLAYOFFS

Even though they rolled into the Western Conference Playoffs with an eight-game winning streak and were at a physical and artistic peak, the Lakers did not envision dominating or sweeping any of their familiar rivals. The West had been deep and powerful all season, with Midwest Division champion San Antonio finishing with the league's best record (58-24), and Sacramento leading the Pacific Division most of the season before getting overtaken by the Lakers (56-26) at the finish.

To get back to the Finals and defend their crown, the Lakers saw nothing but trouble on the horizon, but, as it turned out, it was an illusion of great proportions for the Lakers; and of even more monstrous proportions for the West.

FIRST ROUND

The Lakers quickly sent a message to Portland that this season would be much different than last, when the Blazers nearly beat the Lakers in the Western Finals. The Lakers were aggressive inside with everyone from Rick Fox and Horace Grant (above and right) to the unstoppable force of Shaquille O'Neal (left) dominating the Blazers inside and outside. The Blazers were eliminated in three consecutive games.

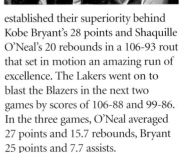

Realistically, the Lakers were thinking survival, not sweep, as they prepared for their best-of-five collision with Portland. Too fresh in everyone's mind was Game 7 of the conference finals one year earlier, when the Blazers led by 15 with 10:28 left in the fourth quarter, only to let the game, series and championship quest get away.

Revenge was the theme for Portland when it came to STAPLES Center, but the Lakers quickly and emphatically established their superiority behind Kobe Bryant's 28 points and Shaquille O'Neal's 20 rebounds in a 106-93 rout that set in motion an amazing run of excellence. The Lakers went on to blast the Blazers in the next two games by scores of 106-88 and 99-86. In the three games, O'Neal averaged 27 points and 15.7 rebounds, Bryant 25 points and 7.7 assists.

"They couldn't stop us," Shaq said. "We want to win another title, and this was the first step."

There were concerns that a weeklong break between series would bring rust, but the Lakers rode to a 108-105 home decision in Game 1 over Sacramento behind the overwhelming force of O'Neal, who had 44 points and 21 rebounds. It was a repeat in Game 2, with Shaq Diesel overpowering the Kings in a 96-90 victory with 43 points and 20 rebounds. It marked the first time in league playoff history that a player had enjoyed 40-20 games back-to-back.

The Kings got a break in Game 3 when O'Neal ran into early foul trouble, but Bryant seized control of the offense with 36 points while O'Neal grabbed 18 rebounds in a 103-81 verdict. Game 4 proved to be the Kobe Show, as the 22-year-old guard produced career highs in points (48) and rebounds (16) to put away the Kings, 119-113, as O'Neal once again was hindered by fouls.

Derek Fisher (20 points) played superbly alongside Bryant in the backcourt.

"We needed to be challenged," Bryant said. "I felt like we needed a gut check going to San Antonio."

O'Neal averaged 33.3 points and 17.3 rebounds, Bryant 35 points and nine rebounds in the second consecutive sweep.

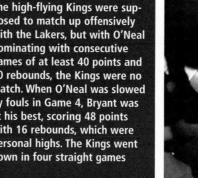

The high-flying Kings were supposed to match up offensively with the Lakers, but with O'Neal dominating with consecutive games of at least 40 points and 20 rebounds, the Kings were no match. When O'Neal was slowed by fouls in Game 4, Bryant was at his best, scoring 48 points with 16 rebounds, which were personal highs. The Kings went down in four straight games

CONFERENCE SEMIFINALS

LAKERS/KINGS

CONFERENCE FINALS

LAKERS/SPURS

This was billed as the showdown of Goliaths — San Antonio's '99 league kings, led by Twin Towers Duncan and Robinson, challenging the 2000 champs.

Game 1 at the Alamodome belonged to a mid-sized model, the electric Bryant. Kobe blazed, soared and roared to 45 points — the most ever surrendered by San Antonio in a postseason game — in a 104-90

conquest that seemed to knock the wind out of the Spurs. Unable to find any answers for Bryant, who came back with a 28-point effort, the Spurs fell 88-81 in Game 2. Duncan had scored 28 and 40 in the two games but was heading to L.A. in an 0-2 hole.

"This team is really hungry," said Phil Jackson. "They are experienced. They are playoff-hardened in some ways. They know momentum

is a big part of the game, especially in the playoffs. The good teams find a way to win on the road."

Game 3 was over before the Spurs knew what hit them. Bryant (36 points, nine rebounds, eight assists) and O'Neal (35 points, 17 rebounds) were simply too much in a 111-72 blowout that ended with an eight-point fourth quarter by the staggered Spurs. They vowed to make it respectable in Game 4, but

the Lakers unleashed a balanced attack featuring Fisher (28 points, with 6 of 7 from three-point range and 11 of 13 overall), O'Neal (26 points, 10 rebounds) and Bryant (24 points, 11 assists) in a 111-82 romp that sent the Spurs home. Fisher was an amazing 15 of 20 from beyond the arc in the series.

"The roll they're on is ridiculous," Spurs coach Gregg Popovich said. "They're awesome."

Bryant quickly took control of the conference finals with 45 points in San Antonio and the Lakers wrestled control of the home-court advantage. Tim Duncan (lower left) had an outstanding series, but the swarming Lakers defensive befuddled the rest of the Spurs as the Lakers again swept a series. They entered the NBA Finals with a record of 11-0 in the playoffs.

"THE ROLL THEY'RE ON IS RIDICULOUS, THEY'RE AWESOME."

— GREGG POPOVICH —

NEW YORK

MIAMI

UTAH

PORTLAND

MILWAUKEE

CHARLOTTE

TORONTO

ORLANDO

DALLAS

While the Lakers were reducing the powerhouse Western Conference to dust during the playoffs, Eastern Conference players performed in a manner so sensational that they earned the ultimate accolade:

There truly is life after Michael Jordan . . . and Magic Johnson and Larry Bird and Julius Erving and all the great stars who contributed to the global popularity of the NBA.

The pyrotechnics started in Game 2 of the Toronto-Philadelphia semifinals series when regular-season MVP Allen Iverson led Philadelphia to series-tying victory with a team playoff record 54-point explosion, which is monumental since a guy named Wilt Chamberlain played for the Sixers. Not to be outdone, Vince Carter responded in Game 3, with 50 points, marking the first time in NBA history that opposing players

scored 50 or more points in the same playoff series. En route to a 4-3 series win, Iverson one-upped Carter by scoring 52 in Game 5 as the Sixers took a 3-2 series lead.

"The Little Kid is playing like the Most Valuable Player," Sixers coach Larry Brown said. "He's playing at a high level on both ends of the floor."

Iverson took the Sixers all the way to the NBA Finals, but discovered

that what had been said all season was, in fact, true. The West was clearly the stronger conference, and the Lakers entered the Finals without a playoff loss. So when the Lakers steamrolled their way to their second consecutive title, it was no surprise.

There were, however, surprises at many levels in Playoffs 2001, although with some teams, the surprises were not of a pleasant nature.

THE CONTENDERS

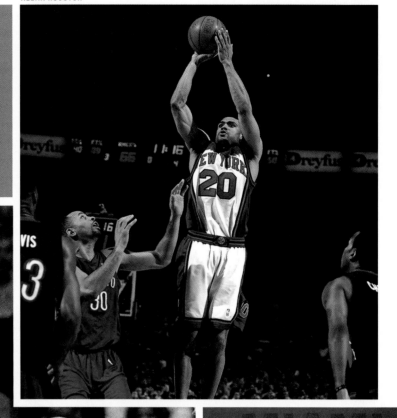

NEW YORK

For the first time since 1984-85 the Knicks started the season without center Patrick Ewing who had been traded to Seattle. New York was led by the perimeter All-Star tandem of Latrell Sprewell and Allan Houston. And while they reached the postseason for the 14th consecutive season, Toronto made sure the Knicks wouldn't get past the first round for the first time since 1991, defeating the Knicks in five games. "They really outworked us," Houston said. "Their strength was their rebounding and they simply overpowered us."

MIAMI

When Alonzo Mourning returned to the Miami Heat near the end of the season after sitting out with a kidney illness, it was more than a symbolic gesture. Mourning was back to help the surprising Heat make a run in the playoffs. But with point guard Tim Hardaway hurting, and Jamal Mashburn burning his old team, Charlotte swept the higher-seeded Heat in the first round. "It was no contest; we were outcoached, outran, outjumped, everything," Coach Pat Riley said.

FIVE

JOHN STOCKTON

UTAH

For much of the season, the play of Karl Malone and John Stockton belied their ages. Led by the future Hall of Famers, the Jazz won 53 games, earning the fourth seed in the Western Conference. The Jazz won the first two games in its first-round series against an inexperienced Dallas team. But then, the younger, fresher Mavericks overwhelmed the aging Jazz, as it dropped three straight for an early playoff exit.

KARL MALONE

DERRICK COLEMAN AND ALONZO MOURNING

PORTLAND

The Trail Blazers desperately wanted to avoid another loss to the Lakers after blowing a big fourth-quarter lead in the deciding game of the 2000 Western Finals. Portland added to its All-Star cast by bringing in Dale Davis and Shawn Kemp. A late-season swoon dropped Portland from a likely No. 1 seed to No. 7 and an unfortunate meeting with a streaking Lakers team. The result: An embarrassing first round as they were swept by the Lakers.

CHARLOTTE

Charlotte rode the reemergence of Jamal Mashburn (20.1 points per game) into a No. 1 option and the maturation of point guard Baron Davis (7.3 assists per game) to a 46-win season. But it was in the postseason that the Hornets had their coming-out party as they swept veteran-laden and playoff-tested Miami in the first round and then drove the Bucks to a seventh game in the Eastern Conference Semifinals before bowing out.

ALLEN IVERSON, GLENN ROBINSON AND TYRONE HILL

SAM CASSELL

MILWAUKEE

Milwaukee's Big Three of Ray Allen, Glenn Robinson and Sam Cassell brushed off a slow start to combine for 62.2 points per game, as they led the Bucks to their first division title since 1985-86. Riding the Big Three, the Bucks stormed past Orlando in the first round of the playoffs and then defeated Charlotte in a tough seven-game series. Their season ended prematurely when they were unable to get past MVP Allen Iverson and the 76ers in the conference finals.

VINCE CARTER

ANTONIO DAVIS

VINCE CARTER

TORONTO

Raptors fans witnessed the revolution of Vince Carter from high-flying phenom to a clutch playoff performer. After being swept by the Knicks in the first round of last season's play-offs and losing Game 1 of this season's first-round matchup, Carter responded by averaging 27 points in three victories as the Raptors won their first playoff series 3-2. From there, Carter moved on to his duel for the ages with Allen Iverson.

ORLANDO

Once Grant Hill was lost for the season, some of the Orlando faithful may have been looking forward to next season, except they overlooked two factors: the emergence of Tracy McGrady and rookie Mike Miller. McGrady developed into a go-to star and Miller walked away with the Rookie of the Year award. McGrady averaged 33.8 points in the playoffs, which led all scorers heading into the Finals. Together, they led Doc Rivers' team into the postseason, where, as in the regular season, they had no answer for the Milwaukee Bucks.

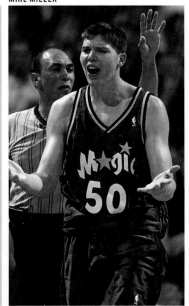

MIKE MILLER

MICHAEL FINLEY

ERVIN JOHNSON AND TRACY McGRADY

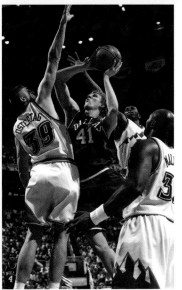

GREG OSTERTAG AND DIRK NOWITZKI [41]

DALLAS

The Reunion Rowdies hadn't seen a Mavericks team this good since Rolando Blackman, Derek Harper and Mark Aguirre were donning uniforms. Led by the triumvirate of Michael Finley, Dirk Nowitzki and Steve Nash, and aided by the midseason addition of Juwan Howard, the Mavericks won 53 games, reached the playoffs for the first time since 1990 and then shocked the basketball world by coming back from an 0-2 deficit to upset Utah in the first round.

THE FINALS

THE DIFFERENCE BETWEEN THE WAY THE LOS ANGELES LAKERS AND
PHILADELPHIA 76ERS ENTERED THE FINALS WAS THE DIFFERENCE
BETWEEN DRAG RACING AND DEMOLITION DERBY. THE LAKERS BLASTED
TO AN 11-0 RECORD, SWEEPING PHOENIX, SACRAMENTO AND SAN
ANTONIO. THE 76ERS TOOK FOUR GAMES TO DEFEAT EIGHTH-SEEDED
INDIANA, AND THEN WERE EXTENDED TO SEVEN GAMES EACH BY
TORONTO AND MILWAUKEE. THE LAKERS ARRIVED AT THE FINALS WITH
THE TOP DOWN, WIND BLOWING IN THEIR HAIR, RELAXED AND CONFIDENT.
THE SIXERS WERE FULL OF DENTS, HAD A COUPLE OF FLAT TIRES, BAGS
UNDER THEIR EYES AND A FRANTIC SORT OF DESPERATION THAT WOULD
SERVE THEM WELL ... AT LEAST FOR ONE GAME.

> *"It wasn't the Lakers that said they were going to sweep us. It was [reporters] who wrote in your scriptures day after day saying that we were going to be swept. But we have been in it night after night with injuries and everything because we have strong heart. I don't know why people were trying to write us off."*

DIKEMBE MUTOMBO

Game

JUNE 6, 2001

ONE

76ERS 107 | LAKERS 101 (OT)

A man who understands the enormity of the NBA Finals stood on the STAPLES Center court one day before it would become center stage for the greatest basketball event in the world . . . and described how it was a perfect fit for Allen Iverson. Maurice Cheeks, the 1980s quintessential point guard who directed the Philadelphia 76ers of Julius Erving and Moses Malone to the 1983 title, said that Iverson wouldmove seamlessly into the global spotlight.

"Nobody can intimidate Allen Iverson," said Cheeks, who now assists Philadelphia 76ers head coach Larry Brown. "He loves playing, loves competition, loves getting hit. He's always able to get back up. When he gets hit the hardest, he gets back up and comes right back at you. He's unique. I've never seen a player like him, his size, with the offensive ability he has. There's no one like Allen. Isiah Thomas was similar in offensive ability, two guys who can put the ball on the floor and shoot from long range, but I think Allen's range is a little deeper than Isiah's was. And Allen's a little more feisty to me than Isiah. Isiah did it a little more subtly than Allen. Allen just attacks you, all night long."

To the surprise of no one who'd watched "The Answer" career through his odyssey from nearly being traded to Detroit during the offseason to the NBA's 2000-2001 Most Valuable Player, he came out firing in Game 1 — and didn't stop until the smoke had cleared in overtime, and the 76ers had rocked the Lakers' world, 107-101. Iverson had 48 points, the most by any player in a Finals debut.

Shaquille O'Neal tried to rally his team with an overpowering individ-

ual performance (44 points, 20 rebounds), but the Man of Steel didn't get enough help from his Super Friends on this occasion. An offense that had been running like an Indy car sputtered against a pressure defense orchestrated by Brown, a master at preparing a team for big games.

Put to bed were all those beautiful Southern California dreams of the Lakers becoming the first team ever to sweep through a post-season unscathed. Their 64-day winning streak — 11 in the postseason, 19 going back to the regular season — was history.

"I just think it's opened up our eyes that we are not invincible," Robert Horry said.

Unfortunately for Horry, he found that out in a very personal way. With 2:40 left in over-time, Horry committed an offensive foul that opened the Philly floodgates after the Lakers had seized a 99-94 lead. The Sixers outscored L.A. 13-2 from that point, with Iverson delivering seven consecutive points around critical baskets by CBA recruit Raja Bell and Eric Snow.

"That was the biggest shot of my career," Snow said of his 17-foot jumper that finished off the Lakers with 10.5 seconds left.

The Lakers would now have to set their sights on Cheeks' 1982-83 champion from Philadelphia, who lost only once on their way to a championship they claimed at the expense of the "Showtime" Lakers with a four-game Finals sweep.

"I'm kind of relieved it's over, in some ways," Phil Jackson said of the streak. "It puts pressure on us to win [Game 2] on our home court. Yeah, the streak was great. Now it's time to get back to the business of playing ball in this series."

Iverson relaxed with a newspaper before the game but then erupted in the first half with 30 points on 11 of 24 marksmanship and 7 of 7 from the foul line.

Whether it was sliding past Kobe Bryant (above) or using his 165-pound body to muscle to the basket against Rick Fox (right), Iverson was the catalyst who lifted the Sixers after they had fallen behind 18-5. His 10 points during a 17-5 run brought the Sixers to within 23-22 starting the second quarter. In a zone now, he rang up 18 points in the second period to send his team surging to its 56-50 halftime advantage.

"WE GOT HEART. WE'RE GOING TO PLAY WITH THAT FIRST. PLAY
WITH TALENT SECOND ... I'VE BEEN WAITING FOR THIS
OPPORTUNITY ALL MY LIFE. I'M NOT THINKING ABOUT FATIGUE.
FATIGUES ARE ARMY CLOTHES."

ALLEN IVERSON

While Iverson was making things happen offensively, Mutombo was a presence befitting the NBA's Defensive Player of the Year. The 7-2 center blocked five shots, and collected 16 rebounds in 44 minutes. It was while Mutombo sat during the third quarter with foul trouble that the Lakers surged back into the game, cutting a 15-point deficit to two with O'Neal reeling off 18 points in the period. But the Sixers held their ground as Mutombo and Iverson demonstrated that they would be no pushover.

The most effective Laker on Iverson was Tyronn Lue, who had averaged only 5.8 minutes in the playoffs but played 22 minutes in Game 1. During the week, Lue had played the role of Iverson in practice. Lue went to Nebraska, where he ended his career as the seventh leading scorer in school history with 1,577 points. So he knows how to score. The practice seemed to serve him well, because Lue attached himself to Iverson and would not let go, although Iverson was so relentless that he wore him down. "Ty added some speed and energy to the game," Jackson said. Bryant (below) also spent time trying to stop Iverson, but Iverson's quickness gave him advantage. Bryant admitted that Lue was more effective. "There were two Ferraris out there, two speedsters," Bryant said. "Ty doesn't get tired. He can run all night. He stopped Iverson from getting to the speed spots. He did a good job."

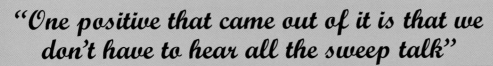

"One positive that came out of it is that we don't have to hear all the sweep talk"

KOBE BRYANT

Bryant entered the game averaging 31.6 points, but managed only 15 points on 7-of-22 from the field. That left Shaq to provide the offense, and he did his part, scoring 44 points, while getting 20 rebounds. He even matched Bryant with five assists. While Mutombo contested shots and made Shaq work, Shaq was not to be denied. Mutombo was in foul trouble in the third quarter, but still managed to finish the game. But, Shaq was an unstoppable force, and by the end of the game, he seemed to be seeking help wherever he could find it. But it never came.

The Sixers subs were efficient, hitting 12 of 19 shots and outscoring the Lakers bench 29-15. Matt Geiger (left) had been a forgotten man, missing eight playoff games with quadriceps tendinitis and not playing in three others by coach's decision. In Game 1, he rose to the challenge, playing a playoff-high 14 minutes and scoring 10 points. Of course, he fouled out trying to cover Shaq, but his contribution was invaluable. Same with Eric Snow (above), who played 31 minutes had had 13 points, five assists and four rebounds; and Raja Bell (right), who played 19 minutes, hit both of the shots he took and added four rebounds.

GAME ONE

76ERS PLAYER	POS	MIN	FGM-A	3PM-A	FTM-A	REBOUNDS OFF	DEF	TOT	AST	PF	ST	TO	BS	PTS
Tyrone Hill	F	40	1-6	0-0	2-2	1	5	6	0	3	0	3	1	4
Jumaine Jones	F	11	2-3	0-1	0-0	0	0	0	0	1	0	0	1	4
Dikembe Mutombo	C	44	4-7	0-0	5-7	5	11	16	0	5	0	0	5	13
Allen Iverson	G	52	18-41	3-8	9-9	2	3	5	6	0	5	3	0	48
Aaron McKie	G	51	3-7	1-1	2-2	2	5	7	9	1	2	5	1	9
Eric Snow		31	5-10	0-1	3-3	0	4	4	5	2	0	5	0	13
Raja Bell		19	2-2	0-0	2-2	1	3	4	1	2	2	1	0	6
Matt Geiger		14	5-7	0-0	0-0	0	0	0	0	6	0	1	1	10
Todd MacCulloch		2	0-0	0-0	0-0	0	0	0	0	1	0	0	0	0
Kevin Ollie		1	0-0	0-0	0-0	0	0	0	0	0	0	0	0	0
George Lynch		DNP												
Rodney Buford		DNP												
TOTAL		265	40-83	4-11	23-25	11	31	42	21	21	10	18	8	107
			(48.2)	(36.4)	(92.0)	Team Rebs:7 Total TO:19 (19 Pts)								

LAKERS PLAYER	POS	MIN	FGM-A	3PM-A	FTM-A	REBOUNDS OFF	DEF	TOT	AST	PF	ST	TO	BS	PTS
Rick Fox	F	44	7-12	3-6	2-2	1	6	7	5	3	2	4	1	19
Horace Grant	F	27	3-11	0-0	2-2	4	1	5	0	1	1	2	2	8
Shaquille O'Neal	C	52	17-28	0-0	10-22	6	14	20	5	3	1	4	0	44
Kobe Bryant	G	52	7-22	0-0	1-1	0	3	3	5	4	1	6	3	15
Derek Fisher	G	23	0-4	0-1	0-0	0	0	0	1	3	1	0	0	0
Robert Horry		27	1-5	1-3	0-0	3	1	4	1	5	2	1	2	3
Tyronn Lue		22	2-3	1-1	0-0	0	1	1	3	2	5	1	1	5
Brian Shaw		18	3-5	1-2	0-0	2	2	4	3	1	1	1	0	7
Devean George		DNP												
Greg Foster		DNP												
Mark Madsen		DNP												
Ron Harper		DNP												
TOTAL		265	40-90	6-13	15-27	16	28	44	23	22	14	19	9	101
			(44.4)	(46.2)	(55.6)	Team Rebs: 14 Total TO: 19 (25 Pts)								

Iverson found talk of a Lakers sweep hilarious. "I'm glad nobody bet their life on it, or they'd be dead now," he said.

Game

JUNE 8, 2001

TWO

LAKERS 98 / 76ERS 89

Larry Brown thought he had already seen the real Shaquille O'Neal. Brown, the Sixers coach, had properly expressed awe, **paying homage to the one-man destruction force whose super powers reduced otherwise mighty men to mere mortals. O'Neal's 44 points and 20 rebounds in the Lakers' Game 1 loss provided Brown with ample evidence that the lofty regard Brown had for Shaq was well deserved.**

And then there was Game 2, which the Sixers were hoping against hope to steal and somehow go home with two victories on the Lakers home court.

It was not to be. Shaq ended the night with 28 points, 20 rebounds, nine assists and eight blocked shots to lead the Lakers to a 98-89 victory.

"Shaq, again, was phenomenal — like he always is," Brown said, having watched the Lakers' 330-pound centerpiece come within one assist and two blocked shots of the first quadruple-double in NBA playoff history.

Unlike Game 1, O'Neal received ample superstar support from Kobe Bryant, who had 31 points, eight rebounds, six assists, two blocks and two steals, winning his duel with Allen Iverson and erasing the bitter taste of an uncharacteristic 15-point effort in Game 1. Bryant was dynamic and dazzling, throwing down spectacular dunks and hitting soft jumpers. Fellow guard Derek Fisher rebounded from a scoreless Game 1 with 14 points, including the three biggest of the game. But this was O'Neal's show. Whatever the

Lakers needed in the course of a 98-89 victory that evened the series at 1-1, their big captain was prepared to take care of it.

"I thought Kobe had a sensational game," Brown said. "But as great as Kobe is, when you have a player in the middle we all have to pay attention to, it opens it up for everybody. I said this the other night. He is not only a great scorer in the post, he's a tremendous passer. That's what you get; you've got to take some poison. He made some unbelievable plays."

The 76ers, with solid bench play from Eric Snow, Todd MacCulloch and Raja Bell, made the Lakers perspire after the Lakers had breezed to a 13-point lead in the fourth quarter. But Shaq picked up his fifth foul with 6:38 to go, and the Sixers quickly went on a 7-0 run that did not end until Brian Shaw hit a three-pointer.

As Philly moved to within three 89-86, Shaq forced a double team, getting the ball deep in the paint. When Iverson collapsed on Shaq, Fisher was alone beyond the three-point arc. O'Neal fed him, and the compactly built lefty broke the Sixers' hearts.

"Biggest play of the game," Brown called Fisher's three-point bomb, and then said: "We scared them a little bit. I loved the way we played, but we're playing against the best team in the NBA with an unbelievable player in Shaquille, who makes everybody better. I'm sitting here and I'm pretty proud of my team. It's a competitive series, regardless of the outcome."

Although O'Neal had 28 points and grabbed 20 rebounds for the second consecutive game, it was his overall effort, especially on defense, that earned the admiration of both coaches after the game. Shaq came within one assist and two blocks of the first quadruple-double in Finals history and was very much in control of the paint all night, as the Sixers' Todd MacCulloch discovered. "I thought Shaq was a dramatically better defensive player in this game," Lakers coach Phil Jackson said. O'Neal's eight blocks tied him with Bill Walton, Hakeem Olajuwon and Patrick Ewing for the Finals record.

After scoring only 15 points while missing 15 of 22 shots in Game 1, Bryant was determined to be a force in Game 2. He was effective from the outside and also attacked the basket with more determination, and success. Bryant led all scorers with 31 points. "From the beginning of the game," said Sixers guard Aaron McKie, who had six rebounds and six assists to go with 14 points, "he wanted to establish himself. He was aggressive, he made shots. That's his job; that's what he gets paid the big bucks to do."

After scoring 48 points in his NBA Finals debut, which was the best opening performance in the history of championship play, Iverson found considerable company every time he went to the basket. He was held to 10 of 29 shooting and scored only 23 points. That ended his streak of three consecutive games of scoring more than 40 points.

The Lakers led by 13 at the halfway point of the fourth quarter, but Sixers coach Larry Brown continued to counsel his troops, in this case Raja Bell and Allen Iverson, and told them to continue chipping at the lead. The Sixers reduced the deficit to three points before succumbing. "What we have to realize is this team's not gonna die," Kobe Bryant said of the Sixers. "They don't ever stop coming at you. You have to respect that. They play all the way through the buzzer. It doesn't make any sense for us to go for the dagger or go for the kill. Instead, we play the possession out, milk it, get easy opportunities and do it that way."

Although Aaron McKie had a chipped bone in his right ankle and still had to guard Bryant, he still remained aggressive and played through the pain, even attacking the basket when he had a chance, although, as all the other Sixers discovered, there was Shaq resistance.

After a huge series against the Spurs in the conference finals, Derek Fisher struggled with no points while Allen Iverson was scoring 48 in Game 1. Fisher, however, was much more aggressive in Game 2, attacking the basket early and then making a three-point shot late in the game after the Sixers had trimmed a 13-point fourth-quarter Laker lead to three points. "Biggest shot of the game," said Sixers coach Larry Brown. Fisher ended the game with 14 points.

While Bryant increased his scoring from 15 points in Game 1 to 31, all aspects of his complete game were on display. Knowing a sure thing when he sees it, Bryant found an open O'Neal for a sure two points — and he looked great while doing it. Bryant ended the night with eight rebounds, six assists, two blocks and two steals.

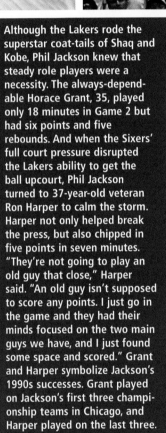

Although the Lakers rode the superstar coat-tails of Shaq and Kobe, Phil Jackson knew that steady role players were a necessity. The always-dependable Horace Grant, 35, played only 18 minutes in Game 2 but had six points and five rebounds. And when the Sixers' full court pressure disrupted the Lakers ability to get the ball upcourt, Phil Jackson turned to 37-year-old veteran Ron Harper to calm the storm. Harper not only helped break the press, but also chipped in five points in seven minutes. "They're not going to play an old guy that close," Harper said. "An old guy isn't supposed to score any points. I just go in the game and they had their minds focused on the two main guys we have, and I just found some space and scored." Grant and Harper symbolize Jackson's 1990s successes. Grant played on Jackson's first three championship teams in Chicago, and Harper played on the last three.

GAME TWO

76ERS PLAYER	POS	MIN	FGM-A	3PM-A	FTM-A	OFF	DEF	TOT	AST	PF	ST	TO	BS	PTS
Tyrone Hill	F	22	1-3	0-0	0-0	1	4	5	0	5	0	0	3	2
Jumaine Jones	F	15	1-2	1-1	0-0	0	3	3	0	1	0	0	1	3
Dikembe Mutombo	C	36	5-12	0-0	6-6	4	9	13	1	3	1	1	1	16
Allen Iverson	G	47	10-29	3-10	0-4	0	4	4	3	3	1	3	0	23
Aaron McKie	G	40	6-17	2-4	0-2	4	2	6	6	3	2	2	0	14
Eric Snow		28	4-9	0-0	4-4	1	1	2	4	1	2	3	0	12
Raja Bell		18	0-1	0-0	2-6	0	2	2	1	3	3	1	0	2
Todd MacCulloch		16	5-9	0-0	3-4	3	2	5	0	3	0	1	0	13
Matt Geiger		13	2-4	0-0	0-0	1	1	2	0	1	0	0	0	4
Kevin Ollie		4	0-1	0-0	0-0	0	0	0	1	0	0	0	0	0
Rodney Buford		1	0-0	0-0	0-0	0	0	0	0	0	0	0	0	0
George Lynch	DNP													
TOTAL		240	34-87	6-15	15-26	14	28	42	16	23	9	11	5	89
			(39.1)	(40.0)	(57.7)	Team Rebs: 10		Total TO: 11 (13 Pts)						

LAKERS PLAYER	POS	MIN	FGM-A	3PM-A	FTM-A	OFF	DEF	TOT	AST	PF	ST	TO	BS	PTS
Rick Fox	F	28	0-4	0-2	0-0	1	5	6	2	4	0	5	1	0
Horace Grant	F	18	2-7	0-0	2-2	3	2	5	2	0	0	0	2	6
Shaquille O'Neal	C	45	12-19	0-0	4-10	8	12	20	9	5	1	5	8	28
Kobe Bryant	G	47	11-23	1-2	8-8	1	7	8	6	4	2	2	2	31
Derek Fisher	G	34	5-11	2-5	2-2	0	0	0	3	4	2	1	0	14
Robert Horry		26	4-6	0-1	0-0	3	4	7	1	3	1	0	0	8
Brian Shaw		25	1-7	1-5	1-2	0	5	5	5	3	1	2	0	4
Tyronn Lue		10	1-1	0-0	0-0	0	0	0	1	0	1	0	0	2
Ron Harper		7	2-3	0-1	1-2	0	1	1	1	0	0	0	0	5
Devean George	DNP													
Greg Foster	DNP													
Mark Madsen	DNP													
TOTAL		240	38-81	4-16	18-26	15	37	52	29	24	7	16	13	98
			(46.9)	(25.0)	(69.2)	Team Rebs: 11		Total TO: 16 (19 Pts)						

Iverson and Bryant had a lively exchange late in the game, undoubtedly with Bryant suggesting that the universe was back in order while Iverson promised a few more surprises in the games ahead.

Game

JUNE 10, 2001

THREE

LAKERS 96 / 76ERS 91

The 76ers knew what to expect when they advanced to meet the Lakers in the NBA Finals. They knew of the immovable inside object (Shaquille O'Neal) and the stylistic irresistible force (Kobe Bryant).

But Robert Horry's stroke?

With O'Neal sitting down after fouling out and with Bryant struggling to find openings against double teams after a spectacular second-quarter shooting display, the Lakers needed a third party to step forward at crunch time in Game 3 in the din of Philadelphia's First Union Center. Horry was delighted to oblige, draining a three-pointer from the corner for a four-point lead with 47.2 seconds left, then calmly dropping four consecutive free throws to seal a 96-91 victory for a 2-1 series lead.

"I felt like I was back in high school — biggest guy on the floor," Horry said, recalling the distant glory days at Alabama's Andalusia High. "We were all-stars at some time in our careers, so we're all ready to step up when the time comes."

When Shaq fouled out with 2:21 left, he joined Derek Fisher on the bench, the point guard having fouled out 26 seconds earlier. With the Lakers leading by two points, a Shaqless Phil Jackson decided to go small. Rick Fox joined Horry, Bryant, Brian Shaw and Tyronn Lue, with the 6-10 Horry passing for a center.

In response, Philadelphia coach Larry Brown pulled his big man, Dikembe Mutombo, with 1:34 to go, deploying five guards: Allen Iverson, Aaron McKie, Eric Snow, Raja Bell and Kevin Ollie. That meant 6-5 McKie, who'd spent most of the night chasing Bryant around the court, was matched against Horry. On the critical three-pointer, the Sixers doubled Bryant, then were unable to rotate over to Horry after Shaw took a pass from Kobe and found Horry alone on the deep baseline.

"That's a rhythm shot for me," Horry said. "I said, 'Hey, I get my feet set, I'm shooting this.' They got a small lineup, I know other guys can go to the boards, get the rebound. I said, 'Hey, release it. If it's good, it's good. If it's not, get back on D.'"

As it swished through the net, Horry turned toward the silenced crowd and began his retreat to the defensive end.

"Robert Horry stepped into a massive role again," Jackson said. "People who watch this team know it's no surprise. That's the reason he plays fourth quarters for us — his ability to defend and also make key shots."

Bryant led the Lakers with 32 points, 16 coming during an 8 for 11 second-quarter eruption. Iverson held up his end of the duel, producing 21 of his team-high 35 points in the second half as the Sixers gamely tried to rally from a 55-45 halftime deficit before a roaring crowd watching Philadelphia's first Finals game since the 1983 title run. Iverson also collected 12 rebounds for the injury-riddled Sixers.

"We've got heart, too," said Lue, the 6-foot guard who helped harass Iverson into missing 18 of 30 shots. "We just don't brag and boast about how much heart we have. We just go out and play."

Although Robert Horry had averaged fewer than five points a game and had a high game of only 11 points during the playoffs, he was the fourth-quarter catalyst in the Lakers' Game 3 victory. Horry had 12 of his 15 points in the fourth quarter, including a three-pointer from the corner with 47.2 seconds left in the fourth quarter. That increased the Lakers' lead from a point to four at 92-88, and provided them with the cushion they needed. For Horry, making big plays in championship games was not a new experience. With two rings from the Rockets' 1994 and 1995 championships and one from last season, he is a veteran of the big game. "The [no] fear factor comes from in Houston, where we played so many elimination games — the most ever in a Finals run (in '95)," Horry said. "You've got to be fearless. You go out there and do what you need to do."

The overwhelming power of Shaquille O'Neal was matched against the angular Dikembe Mutombo, whose height, long arms, exquisite timing and competitive determination had resulted in four defensive player of the year awards. While O'Neal could not be shut down, Mutombo was a 7-2 pest who refused to back down, which ultimately meant that he got knocked down. Shaq fouled out after scoring 30 points with 12 rebounds and four blocked shots, and he was clearly unhappy with the defensive techniques employed by Mutombo and the 76ers.

"Challenge me," Shaq said, taunting Mutombo. "Treat me like a game of checkers and play me. That's all I'm asking, just play me. Just play. But like I said, you know, I'm playing hard. I'm allowed to pivot. I'm allowed to play strong. I'm allowed to be powerful. That's what I've been doing my whole career and I'm not gonna change that now. So, you know, just play me. Treat me like Sega and play me."

Mutombo and his teammates, meanwhile, were irritated by the barbs from Shaq, noting that he had three stitches in his mouth. "This is a war," Mutombo said "We're in the middle of the war." And Mutombo was quick to add that he believed Shaq might be bothered because Mutombo had no fear. "I don't mind getting hit," Mutombo said. "I'm not going to let myself get his 24 hours a day, but I don't get out of the way or get scared. I'm not scared of him at all. He's a man like me. He breathes the same air as me. I lost my fear when I was 2."

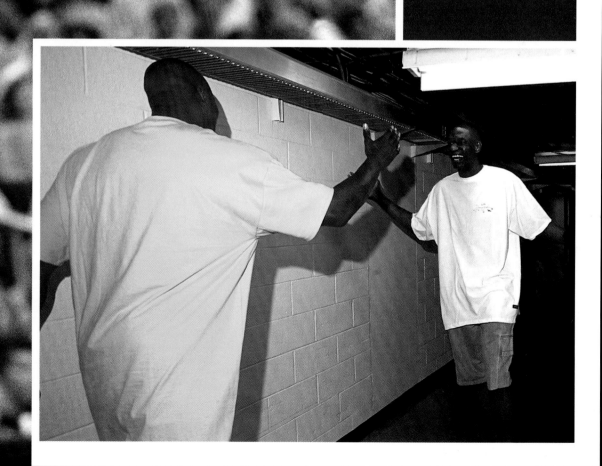

When Shaq finally picked up his sixth foul, he strode to the bench, a very unhappy Goliath. "I think the matchup with Shaq and Dikembe, it's a huge uphill challenge for Shaq," Bryant said. "Dikembe's a four-time defensive player of the year. You know he's going to be ready to play come Game 4 as he has been the other three games. I think Shaq wants to see him play a little bit more straight up, to try to outwit him I guess, instead of flopping. I think he's really excited about the matchup going up against Dikembe. He thought he was going to meet somebody that was going to step up to him, step to the challenge and really make it difficult for him."

As always, Bryant and Iverson provided the pyrotechnics with mad dashes and spectacular finishes at the basket. Bryant had 32 points and six rebounds while Iverson had 35 points and a career-high 12 rebounds despite standing a mere 6-0 in the land of giants. Iverson again struggled from the field, however, making only 12 of 30 shots. Still, afterward he was encouraged despite the 2-1 deficit. "They respect us," Iverson said. "Last series [against San Antonio] they won every game by 20 points. We haven't got blown out one time. Every fourth quarter, we're in the game."

Despite the animated discussion at the end of Game 2, it is clear that Bryant and Iverson, 22 and 26 years old respectively, have a mutual admiration society . . . and a rivalry that promises to last for years.

Mutombo entered the Finals with averages of 13.1 points and 14.2 rebounds, but met the challenge of O'Neal with increased scoring. After three games, Mutombo was averaging 17.3 points and 13.7 rebounds, and had demonstrated a fine shooting touch from 10 feet while also consistently hitting his hook shot. "As great as Shaq played, Dikembe has been as consistent as any player we've had on the court," said Sixers guard Aaron McKie. "And, really, he was the only reason we had a chance to win."

Although Jackson would have preferred to not diagram a strategy that he employed after Shaq fouled out with 2:21 left in the game, he was prepared. Part of his adjustment was to go with a smaller lineup with Bryant, Rick Fox, Brian Shaw and Tyronn Lue. With that lineup, the 6-10 Horry was actually the center and delivered a personal playoff-high 15 points for the Lakers. Horry had been struggling in the playoffs with his stroke, shooting only 31.5 percent from the field and 26.3 from three-point land. His free throw percentage was an abysmal 43.8. But he was perfect when it counted, in the fourth quarter: three of three from the field and four of four from the foul line. "Robert does this all the time," Bryant said. "He's sneaky about it. It's not once in a while, it's consistent. He did it last year in the Finals, he did it for us all regular season long, and he's going to keep on doing it. That's Robert for you."

GAME THREE

LAKERS PLAYER	POS	MIN	FGM-A	3PM-A	FTM-A	OFF	DEF	TOT	AST	PF	ST	TO	BS	PTS
Horace Grant	F	29	2-5	0-0	0-0	3	4	7	1	3	0	0	0	4
Rick Fox	F	22	1-3	0-1	1-2	0	3	3	2	2	3	2	0	3
Shaquille O'Neal	C	41	11-20	0-0	8-9	3	9	12	3	6	0	3	4	30
Kobe Bryant	G	48	13-30	0-2	6-6	0	6	6	3	2	2	2	0	32
Derek Fisher	G	31	2-5	0-1	3-4	1	1	2	2	6	0	1	0	7
Brian Shaw		28	0-3	0-1	0-0	1	4	5	3	3	1	2	0	0
Robert Horry		24	4-5	3-3	4-4	1	3	4	3	2	1	1	2	15
Tyronn Lue		17	2-4	1-2	0-0	1	0	1	1	2	1	1	0	5
Devean George		DNP												
Greg Foster		DNP												
Mark Madsen		DNP												
Ron Harper		DNP												
TOTAL		240	35-75	4-10	22-25	10	30	40	18	26	8	13	6	96
			(46.7)	(40.0)	(88.0)				Team Rebs: 7 Total TO: 13 (8 Pts)					

76ERS PLAYER	POS	MIN	FGM-A	3PM-A	FTM-A	OFF	DEF	TOT	AST	PF	ST	TO	BS	PTS
Tyrone Hill	F	26	1-7	0-0	0-0	0	2	2	0	4	0	1	1	2
Jumaine Jones	F	18	1-2	1-2	0-0	0	1	1	0	1	0	1	0	3
Dikembe Mutombo	C	42	9-14	0-0	5-8	5	7	12	0	4	1	2	2	23
Allen Iverson	G	47	12-30	1-6	10-13	2	10	12	4	1	0	1	1	35
Aaron McKie	G	42	2-8	0-1	1-1	1	5	6	8	1	0	3	2	5
Eric Snow		34	4-11	0-1	6-7	4	2	6	5	4	1	3	0	14
Raja Bell		17	1-5	0-2	0-0	0	2	2	0	3	3	1	0	2
Todd MacCulloch		8	0-0	0-0	0-0	0	0	0	0	0	0	0	0	0
Matt Geiger		5	2-2	0-0	0-0	0	0	0	0	3	0	2	0	4
Kevin Ollie		1	1-1	0-0	1-1	1	0	1	0	1	0	0	0	3
George Lynch		DNP												
Rodney Buford		DNP												
TOTAL		240	33-80	2-12	23-30	13	29	42	17	22	5	14	6	91
			(41.3)	(16.7)	(76.7)				Team Rebs: 8 Total TO: 15 (10 Pts)					

Shaq was subdued afterward, happy that the Lakers had won and regained the home court advantage, yet wary of the resilient Sixers team that promised not to quit.

"I think there's definitely a stronger bond. This year we went through so much. To be able to pull it all together now and to be able to play the way that we're playing, I definitely think there's a stronger bond there. It's like a brotherhood type of feel that we have. I love these guys. I do. I have so much respect for them."

KOBE BRYANT

Game

JUNE 13, 2001

FOUR

LAKERS 100 | 76ERS 86

The first two-day break in the Finals was a veritable gold mine for the 223 members of the international media who were covering the event. Shaquille O'Neal was, as he described it, at his "quotatious" best, spewing out a volcano of colorful words portraying Dikembe Mutombo, the darling of the international media representing 32 countries, as something less than a warrior. O'Neal, in fact, suggested that at worst, Mutombo, who is from the Congo (formerly Zaire) was a very poor actor who took the art of flopping to record low levels.

Shaq later said he was simply being playful, trying to inject a little humor and controversy into the Finals, perhaps, for the benefit of NBC's ratings. But veteran Shaq watchers suggested a more calculated ploy. After fouling out of Game 3, Shaq was intent on physically dominating Game 4, and he wanted to make sure the referees gave him the leeway to do so.

Nothing would stand in his way. O'Neal summoned every ounce of power from his 7-1, 330-pound mass of muscle and dominated Game 4 in the way that few, if any, Finals games had been dominated in NBA history. It wasn't so much the final numbers: 34 points, 14 rebounds and 5 assists. It was the way he did it, relentlessly using his strength to clear the lane while physically overwhelming Mutombo and the Sixers. Each dunk was delivered with grenade-like power. After the 100-86 Lakers victory, the Sixers were as amazed as everyone else. It was a jaw-dropping performance.

"It was a whole lot of Shaquille O'Neal," Allen Iverson said.

"The guy's the best," said Sixers coach Larry Brown. "He's playing against a helluva player in Dikembe, but he's phenomenal. I don't know how one player could do any more than he's done in four games." Kobe Bryant willingly assisted in the Shaq Show, delivering 19 points, 10 rebounds and nine assists. The Lakers were a sizzling 10 for 19 from three-point range, with reserves Robert Horry, Ron Harper, Tyronn Lue and Brian Shaw a combined 7 for 10 from long distance.

"They had a marvelous contribution off their bench," Brown said. "It's pretty tough to beat that team when all things are working their way. Shaq finds people. He's so unselfish."

Mutombo tried to keep O'Neal busy at the defensive end, making nine of 11 shots for 19 points while taking down nine rebounds, but his preoccupation with Shaq took away from his customary disruptive nature defensively. Dikembe, the four-time Defensive Player of the Year, managed to block only one shot as the Lakers hit an even 50 percent from the floor.

"He's a great player," Mutombo said. "All I'm trying to do is show my skill and protect my team by not having him score all those easy baskets. He's going to get his dunk regardless. Nobody ever said that Mutombo's gonna step on the floor and Shaq is not gonna get his dunk."

Five of Shaq's 13 field goals (in 25 attempts) were dunks. Through four games, Shaq had outdunked the whole Sixers team, 18-9. In Game 4, Dikembe actually had outdunked his rival, 6-5. Not that it mattered.

"I'm on a mission this year," O'Neal said. "I got 115 moves on each block. I always go for my first move, and if somebody takes my first move away, I usually beat them to the second move."

O'Neal's brilliance in Game 4 led to the obvious question afterward. A year after winning his first MVP, had he actually gotten better? At 29, was he playing the best basketball of his career? "I would think so," O'Neal said. "I'm much older, much wiser. I have a great teacher in Phil Jackson. I've always had good guidance from my parents. I've always been a good listener. So, this is probably the best that I'm playing. And, hopefully, it gets better as I get older."

Pat Croce, the Sixers' excitable president, was asked about the most difficult part of the series. "What's hard is seeing Shaquille O'Neal on the court," Croce said. "That's what kills me. Every time he gets the ball — and he's playing so great — he knows exactly what to do with it. Either he attacks the basket, or he passes to the open man. It just killed us. He's killing us."

While O'Neal was dominating, Bryant was playing a spectacular all-around game, finishing one assist shy of a triple-double. In the third quarter, the Lakers increased their lead to 18 at 77-59 at the end of the period, and Bryant led the scoring with nine points. He finished with 19 points, 10 rebounds and nine assists.

Once again, veteran Ron Harper lulled the Sixers to sleep in the second quarter, sneaking in with all eight of his points for the night. And Robert Horry, who played a key role in the Game 3 victory, added nine points, including two clutch three-pointers in the fourth quarter when the Sixers were making a run. "They hit big shots all the time," Bryant said. "All the time. It's not just one or two guys. It's not just Robert Horry. It's Ron Harper coming in, hitting a big shot. It's Brian Shaw coming in. It's Tyronn Lue coming in, hitting big shots. They've done that and they've done that consistently. It's not only their shooting but it's the defense, it's the deflections, it's the rebounds. Our bench is unbelievable, to say the least."

True to their Rocky-esque character, the 76ers rattled the Lakers' cage late in the game. They came off the floor, rebounding from a seemingly insurmountable 22-point deficit to make it interesting for their fans with a 13-0 run starting with a Tyrone Hill basket at the end of the third quarter. Iverson scored six of his 35 points during the run, and closed to within 77-70. But the Lakers regained control, and Dikembe Mutombo (19 points) was limited by foul troubles. The Sixers had again shown a lot of heart, but Coach Larry Brown found it difficult to find any solace in a moral victory. "We keep talking about heart and character and stuff like that," Brown said. "Well, it's past that. We've got to figure out a way to win. We've just got to remember that we could have packed it in, down 20-something in the fourth quarter, and we didn't, and we got to build on that.

When the Sixers moved close in the last period, Shaq came back into the game, quickly threw down a slam dunk, courtesy of Lue, then pitched it out to Shaw for a three-pointer. Another trey by Lue completed an 8-0 run that took the life out of the 76ers and their partisan crowd. "I had an inkling we were going to play a game like that tonight," Jackson said. "We were a very determined team when we came to work this week. Shaq was true to his promise. He played the kind of game we wanted. He played the game right. They surrounded him real quick, and he had to make some real quick moves to free himself."

Iverson, as usual, tried to drive the 76ers with his will and offensive creativity. With the Lakers and Tyronn Lue constantly hounding him, Iverson was able to hit only 12 of 30 shots while making 10 of 14 from the foul line. As he noted afterward, his 35 points carried nothing close to the impact of O'Neal's 34. "He's the most dominant on both ends of the court," Iverson said. "He means so much to that team. He's just too big, too strong. I mean, I've never seen anything this dominant."

Brian Shaw played only 10 minutes, but seemed energetic, contributing five points, including a key three-pointer that helped quell the Sixers' fourth-quarter comeback. For Shaw, it was the end of an active 48-hour period. He flew to Oakland after Game 3 to be with his wife Nikki, who gave birth to their third child, Bianca Nicole. Shaw took a red-eye flight back to Philly, and admitted that he was dragging before the game when approached by O'Neal. "He saw me kind of nodding off in the corner of the locker room," Shaw said, grinning. "I was trying to stay awake, but I couldn't help myself. He said, `We're gonna need you tonight.' I was a little delirious, to say the least, but I was happy that it was all worthwhile. I got to see the birth of my daughter and we won the game."

GAME FOUR

LAKERS PLAYER	POS	MIN	FGM-A	3PM-A	FTM-A	OFF	DEF	TOT	AST	PF	ST	TO	BS	PTS
Rick Fox	F	30	2-7	1-3	2-2	0	1	1	4	3	0	1	0	7
Horace Grant	F	25	1-4	0-0	0-0	0	5	5	0	2	0	2	2	2
Shaquille O'Neal	C	42	13-25	0-0	8-16	8	6	14	5	4	0	3	0	34
Kobe Bryant	G	43	6-13	0-2	7-12	2	8	10	9	2	1	4	1	19
Derek Fisher	G	34	4-7	2-4	0-0	0	1	1	1	3	3	3	0	10
Robert Horry		24	3-4	3-3	0-0	1	3	4	0	3	0	0	1	9
Ron Harper		16	3-5	1-2	1-1	0	4	4	2	2	1	0	1	8
Tyronn Lue		14	2-3	2-3	0-0	0	1	1	2	0	1	1	0	6
Brian Shaw		10	2-3	1-2	0-1	0	2	2	1	3	0	2	0	5
Mark Madsen		2	0-1	0-0	0-0	1	0	1	0	0	0	0	1	0
Devean George	DNP													
Greg Foster	DNP													
TOTAL		240	36-72	10-19	18-32	12	31	43	24	22	6	14	6	100
			(50.0)	(52.6)	(56.3)	Team Rebs: 13		Total TO: 14 (13 Pts)						

76ERS PLAYER	POS	MIN	FGM-A	3PM-A	FTM-A	OFF	DEF	TOT	AST	PF	ST	TO	BS	PTS
Tyrone Hill	F	21	3-4	0-0	1-1	2	5	7	1	5	0	1	0	7
Jumaine Jones	F	11	0-3	0-0	0-0	1	2	3	1	1	1	0	0	0
Dikembe Mutombo	C	44	9-11	0-0	1-3	3	6	9	0	5	0	1	1	19
Allen Iverson	G	46	12-30	1-4	10-14	1	3	4	4	3	1	2	0	35
Aaron McKie	G	40	1-9	0-2	3-4	0	3	3	2	1	0	1	0	5
Eric Snow		29	5-10	0-0	1-4	0	4	4	4	4	3	1	0	11
Raja Bell		20	0-2	0-0	1-2	0	0	0	1	2	2	1	0	1
Matt Geiger		11	2-4	0-0	2-2	0	2	2	1	4	0	0	0	6
George Lynch		8	0-0	0-0	0-0	0	2	2	1	2	2	0	0	0
Rodney Buford		5	1-3	0-0	0-0	1	2	3	0	0	0	0	0	2
Kevin Ollie		3	0-1	0-0	0-0	0	0	0	0	0	0	0	0	0
Todd MacCulloch		2	0-0	0-0	0-0	0	0	0	0	0	0	1	0	0
TOTAL		240	33-77	1-6	19-30	8	29	37	15	27	9	9	1	86
			(42.9)	(16.7)	(63.3)	Team Rebs: 12		Total TO: 9 (9 Pts)						

After a valiant comeback, Iverson admitted that he was drained and that the 76ers faced a difficult task of winning three consecutive games against a Lakers team that had not lost three straight the entire year. "We know it's like mission impossible," Iverson said. Bryant, meanwhile, was celebrating the spoils of victory, confident that a second championship was not far away.

"Shaq was the dominant player. He was the guy that was the motivator and the energizer for our team. He truly was a great leader. For him to win the second one, I think, this is validation of his greatness. Shaq has got more in him. I expect him to have more than two championships before he's finished with this game."

PHIL JACKSON

Game

JUNE 15, 2001

FIVE

LAKERS 108 | 76ERS 96

The momentous day began for Lakers General Manager Mitch Kupchak with a phone call to Jerry West, his mentor, in Los Angeles. Kupchak left a message on West's answering machine.

"I just wanted to see how he was doing, touch bases with him," Kupchak said. "I wanted Jerry to know I was thinking about him."

West was still in Kupchak's mind hours later as he stood inside a hot, cramped, rowdy dressing room at First Union Center in Philadelphia. **Phil Jackson's Lakers had won their second consecutive NBA championship with a rousing 108-96 Game 5 victory over the 76ers behind the overwhelming dominance of Finals MVP Shaquille O'Neal (29 points, 13 rebounds, five blocks) and all-around brilliance of Kobe Bryant (26 points, 12 rebounds, six assists).**

Allen Iverson went down firing with 37 points in defeat, eclipsing the Finals record for points (178) in a five-game series. The previous record was 169 and belonged to none other than . . . Jerry West, who had set the mark in 1965 with the Lakers.

O'Neal, who had never won a title at any level until last season, was festive in celebrating the victory, unlike last season when he wept with joy after his first title.

"This time it's fun," said O'Neal, who also won his second Finals MVP award. "It's business. I want to thank my teammates for always looking out for me, always throwing me the ball, playing well. I have great teammates. I knew all along if we kept everyone involved, these guys were going to step up for me."

"Surreal," said Jackson, his team having won 23 of its last 24 games. "This one is really surreal."

The Lakers' 15-1 postseason record set an NBA record for playoff winning percentage at .937, erasing the 12-1 and .923 standards set by the 1982-83 Philadelphia 76ers. It was the franchise's eighth title since moving to Los Angeles in 1960 from Minneapolis, where it had won five championships.

"My hope is that he watched this game on TV," Kupchak said of West, who left the Lakers after the 1999-2000 title run, "and somewhere in the middle of the third or fourth quarter, he had a big smile on his face. He should be proud of this team. These were Jerry's guys. He put this team together. There were some testy moments in getting some things done, but at the end of the day, the major pieces were in place, and the credit goes to Jerry West."

O'Neal, 29, and Bryant, 22, are cornerstones that make the Lakers the envy of every other franchise in the league.

O'Neal averaged 33.0 points, 15.8 rebounds and 3.4 blocks in the Finals, rising to the occasion in his showdown with NBA Defensive Player of the Year Dikembe Mutombo.

"I think the matchup showed that we not only have a great center," said Philadelphia coach Larry Brown. "But this guy [O'Neal], he's as good as they get. I've never seen a better player in my life. I mean that. He was phenomenal."

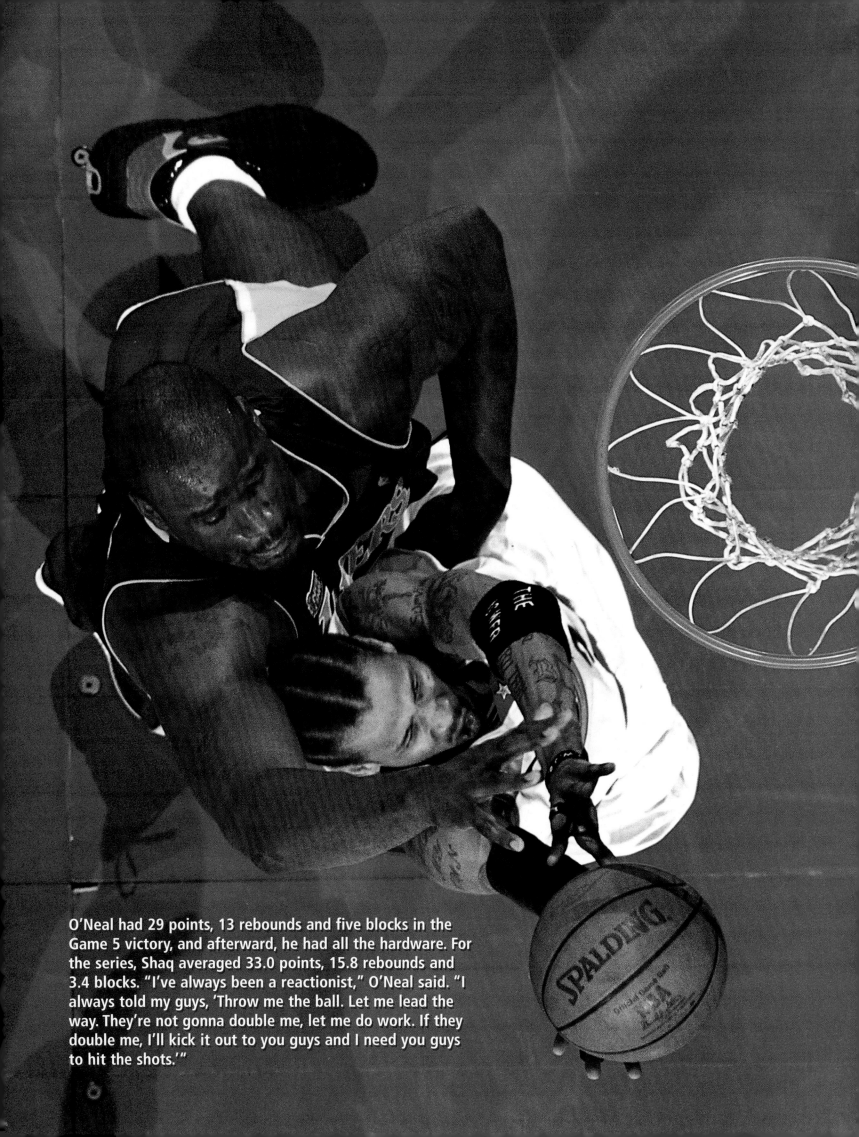

O'Neal had 29 points, 13 rebounds and five blocks in the Game 5 victory, and afterward, he had all the hardware. For the series, Shaq averaged 33.0 points, 15.8 rebounds and 3.4 blocks. "I've always been a reactionist," O'Neal said. "I always told my guys, 'Throw me the ball. Let me lead the way. They're not gonna double me, let me do work. If they double me, I'll kick it out to you guys and I need you guys to hit the shots.'"

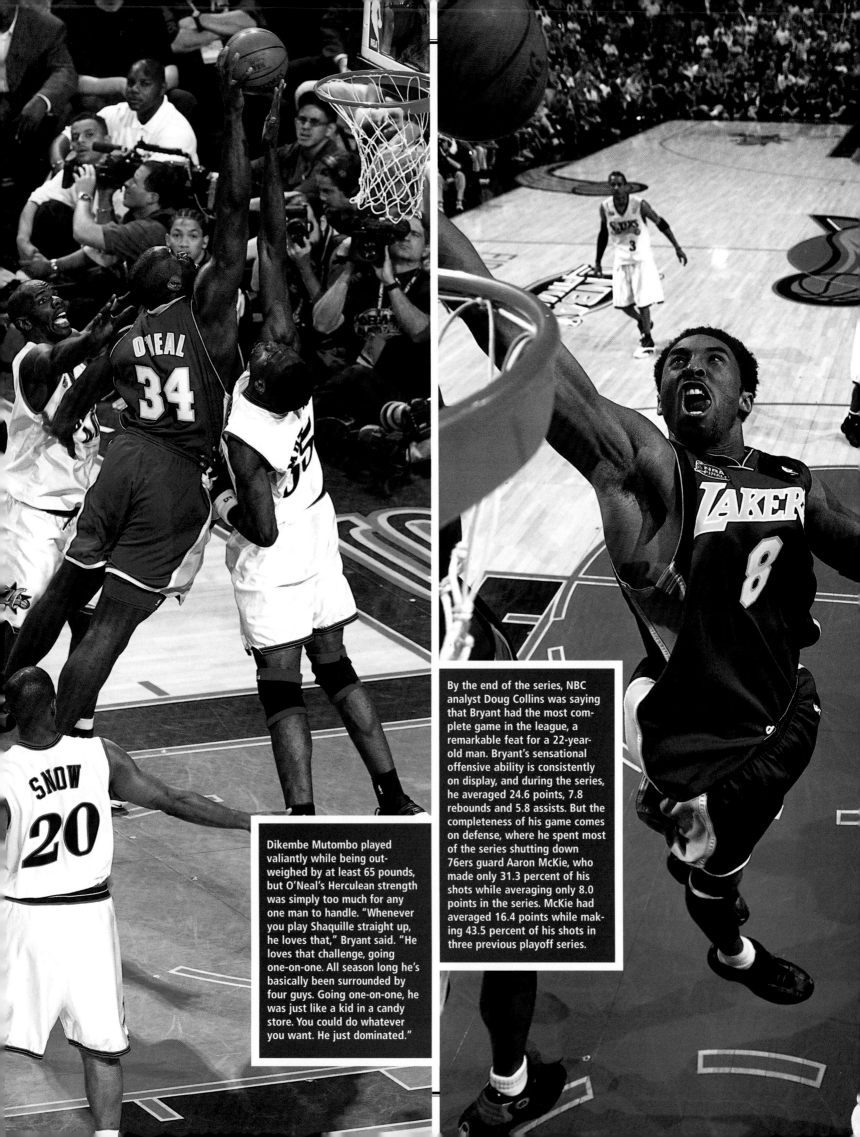

Dikembe Mutombo played valiantly while being out-weighed by at least 65 pounds, but O'Neal's Herculean strength was simply too much for any one man to handle. "Whenever you play Shaquille straight up, he loves that," Bryant said. "He loves that challenge, going one-on-one. All season long he's basically been surrounded by four guys. Going one-on-one, he was just like a kid in a candy store. You could do whatever you want. He just dominated."

By the end of the series, NBC analyst Doug Collins was saying that Bryant had the most complete game in the league, a remarkable feat for a 22-year-old man. Bryant's sensational offensive ability is consistently on display, and during the series, he averaged 24.6 points, 7.8 rebounds and 5.8 assists. But the completeness of his game comes on defense, where he spent most of the series shutting down 76ers guard Aaron McKie, who made only 31.3 percent of his shots while averaging only 8.0 points in the series. McKie had averaged 16.4 points while making 43.5 percent of his shots in three previous playoff series.

Iverson was his usual relentless self, attacking the basket with no regard for his body. A second-period collision with Kobe Bryant resulted in a contusion on his right side, but Iverson was still a warrior, playing 45 minutes. He ended the night with 37 points, but again had difficulties with the Lakers defense as he made only 14 of 32 shots from the field. "This is amazing," said Sixers coach Larry Brown. "Allen told me he thought he cracked some ribs. They X-rayed it, I don't know, they didn't find that. It's what that kid's about. He had a phenomenal year. And I think being in this environment on this stage, people really recognize what an unbelievable competitor he is and what a great player. And I'm happy for him. I think he deserves that. Like I said, we would have never been in this position had it not been for his unbelievable play throughout the whole year."

Lost in the dominant shadow of O'Neal was the offensive performance of Mutombo, who averaged 12.7 points in the first three playoff rounds. Mutombo increased his offensive production to 16.8 points against O'Neal and proved that he could lift his game to new levels.

"Personally, on my side, it was a great challenge," Mutombo said of the matchup with O'Neal. "It was not easy." Sixers coach Larry Brown lauded Mutombo, saying, "Allan Houston mentioned something, that you have to have the best defensive player in the league to play against [O'Neal], and we had it. I think the matchup showed that we not only have a great center, but this guy [Shaq] is as good as they get. And I've never seen a better player in my life."

The Lakers' role players complemented the superstars perfectly. In Game 5, Rick Fox had 20 points and Derek Fisher (opposite page) added 18. The combination of attacking the basket and long-range shooting was effective throughout the series. When the 76ers rallied in the fourth quarter, it was Fisher who drilled a pair of three-point bombs that silenced Brown's gritty team and its rabid fans once and for all. His first trey, with 4:56 left, came after a 10-1 Philadelphia run and gave the Lakers a 94-86 lead. The knockout blow, from 25 feet, made the cushion 103-93 with 51.4 second left. "I couldn't have dreamed of a better ending," said Fisher, who missed the team's first 62 games recovering from a fractured foot. With their hard-nosed southpaw in the lineup, the Lakers were 30-6. Standing on a bench responding to interviewers, Fox saw Kupchak in a corner and shouted, "What about keeping it together, Mitch?" "Absolutely," Kupchak replied. "Absolutely."

RON HARPER

After missing the Lakers title run last season because of injury, Tyronn Lue provided a boost, pestering Iverson throughout the series. Meanwhile, old pros Ron Harper and Robert Horry were in familiar territory. Harper won three titles with the Bulls and Horry had two rings from the Rockets' championship years. They increased their totals to five and four, respectively.

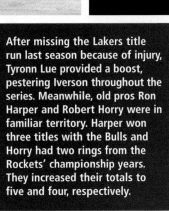

ROBERT HORRY

GAME FIVE

LAKERS PLAYER	POS	MIN	FGM-A	3PM-A	FTM-A	OFF	DEF	TOT	AST	PF	ST	TO	BS	PTS
Rick Fox	F	40	5-8	3-3	7-7	1	5	6	6	2	1	2	0	20
Horace Grant	F	24	2-7	0-0	2-4	3	3	6	0	3	1	0	1	6
Shaquille O'Neal	C	45	10-18	0-0	9-19	6	7	13	2	2	0	5	5	29
Kobe Bryant	G	44	7-18	2-3	10-11	2	10	12	6	3	1	3	1	26
Derek Fisher	G	36	6-12	6-8	0-0	0	3	3	3	4	2	1	1	18
Robert Horry		26	2-5	1-3	2-2	2	4	6	1	4	0	0	2	7
Brian Shaw		12	0-2	0-0	2-2	0	0	0	2	2	1	0	0	2
Tyronn Lue		10	0-1	0-0	0-0	0	1	1	1	2	0	1	0	0
Ron Harper		2	0-0	0-0	0-0	0	0	0	0	0	0	0	0	0
Mark Madsen		1	0-0	0-0	0-0	0	0	0	0	0	0	0	0	0
Devean George	DNP													
Greg Foster	DNP													
TOTAL		240	32-71	12-17	32-45	14	33	47	21	22	6	12	10	108
			(45.1)	(70.6)	(71.1)	Team Rebs: 8			Total TO: 13 (17 Pts)					

76ERS PLAYER	POS	MIN	FGM-A	3PM-A	FTM-A	OFF	DEF	TOT	AST	PF	ST	TO	BS	PTS
Aaron McKie	F	34	3-7	1-1	0-0	0	5	5	5	4	2	3	0	7
Tyrone Hill	F	32	7-13	0-0	4-6	3	10	13	1	4	0	0	1	18
Dikembe Mutombo	C	42	6-11	0-0	1-2	3	8	11	1	6	0	1	2	13
Allen Iverson	G	45	14-32	3-11	6-8	0	3	3	2	5	2	3	0	37
Eric Snow	G	42	4-14	0-1	5-8	6	0	6	12	3	2	2	1	13
Matt Geiger		11	1-1	0-0	0-0	1	0	1	1	6	0	0	0	2
Jumaine Jones		7	0-0	0-0	0-0	1	2	3	0	1	0	0	0	0
Rodney Buford		7	0-3	0-1	0-0	1	2	3	0	2	0	1	0	0
George Lynch		6	1-3	0-0	0-0	2	1	3	0	1	0	0	0	2
Kevin Ollie		6	0-0	0-0	2-2	0	0	0	0	0	0	0	0	2
Raja Bell		5	1-3	0-1	0-0	1	0	1	1	0	0	0	0	2
Todd MacCulloch		3	0-3	0-0	0-0	2	0	2	0	0	0	0	0	0
TOTAL		240	37-90	4-15	18-26	20	31	51	23	32	6	10	4	96
			(41.1)	(26.7)	(69.2)	Team Rebs: 7			Total TO: 11 (15 Pts)					

RECORDS SET AT NBA FINALS 2001
NBA FINALS RECORDS SET FOR 5-GAME SERIES

- Most Points
  178- Allen Iverson, Philadelphia, 2001
  169 – Jerry West, L.A. Lakers, 1965
  165 – Shaquille O'Neal, L.A. Lakers, 2001
  156 – Michael Jordan, Chicago, 1991

- Most Field Goals
  66 – Allen Iverson, Philadelphia, 2001
  63 – Shaquille O'Neal, L.A. Lakers, 2001
  63 – Michael Jordan, Chicago, 1991
  62 – Wilt Chamberlain, San Francisco, 1964

- Most Field Goal Attempts
  162 – Allen Iverson, Philadelphia 76ers, 2001
  139 – Jerry West, L.A. Lakers, 1965
  129 – Paul Arizin, Philadelphia Warriors, 1956

- Most Three-Point Field Goals Made
  11 – Allen Iverson, Philadelphia, 2001
  11 – Isiah Thomas, Detroit, 1990
  9 – Jaren Jackson, San Antonio, 1999
  8 – Robert Horry, L.A. Lakers, 2001

- Most Three-Point Field Goals Attempted
  39 – Allen Iverson, Philadelphia, 2001
  25 – Terry Porter, Portland, 1990
  24 – Jaren Jackson, San Antonio, 1999

- Most Free Throw Attempts
  76 – Shaquille O'Neal, L.A. Lakers, 2001
  60 – Bob Pettit, St. Louis, 1961
  59 – Jerry West, L.A. Lakers, 1965

- Most Offensive Rebounds
  31 – Shaquille O'Neal, L.A. Lakers, 2001
  21 – Elvin Hayes, Washington, 1979
  20 – Dikembe Mutombo, Philadelphia, 2001
  20 – Wes Unseld, Washington, 1979

- Most Blocked Shots
  17 – Shaquille O'Neal, L.A. Lakers, 2001
  16 – Jack Sikma, Seattle, 1979
  15 – David Robinson, San Antonio, 1999
  9 – Dikembe Mutombo, Philadelphia, 2001

- Most Three-Point Field Goals Made, Team
  36 – L.A. Lakers vs. Philadelphia, 2001
  25 – Detroit vs. Portland, 1990
  21 – San Antonio vs. New York, 1999

- Most Three-Point Field Goal Attempts, Team
  75 – L.A. Lakers vs. Philadelphia, 2001
  62 – San Antonio vs. New York, 1999
  56 – Detroit vs. Portland, 1990

- Most Blocked Shots, Team
  44 – L.A. Lakers vs. Philadelphia, 2001
  39 – Seattle vs. Washington, 1979
  29 – San Antonio vs. New York, 1999

- Fewest Turnovers, Team
  64 – Philadelphia vs. L.A. Lakers, 2001
  64 – New York vs. San Antonio, 1999
  66 – Chicago vs. L.A. Lakers, 1991

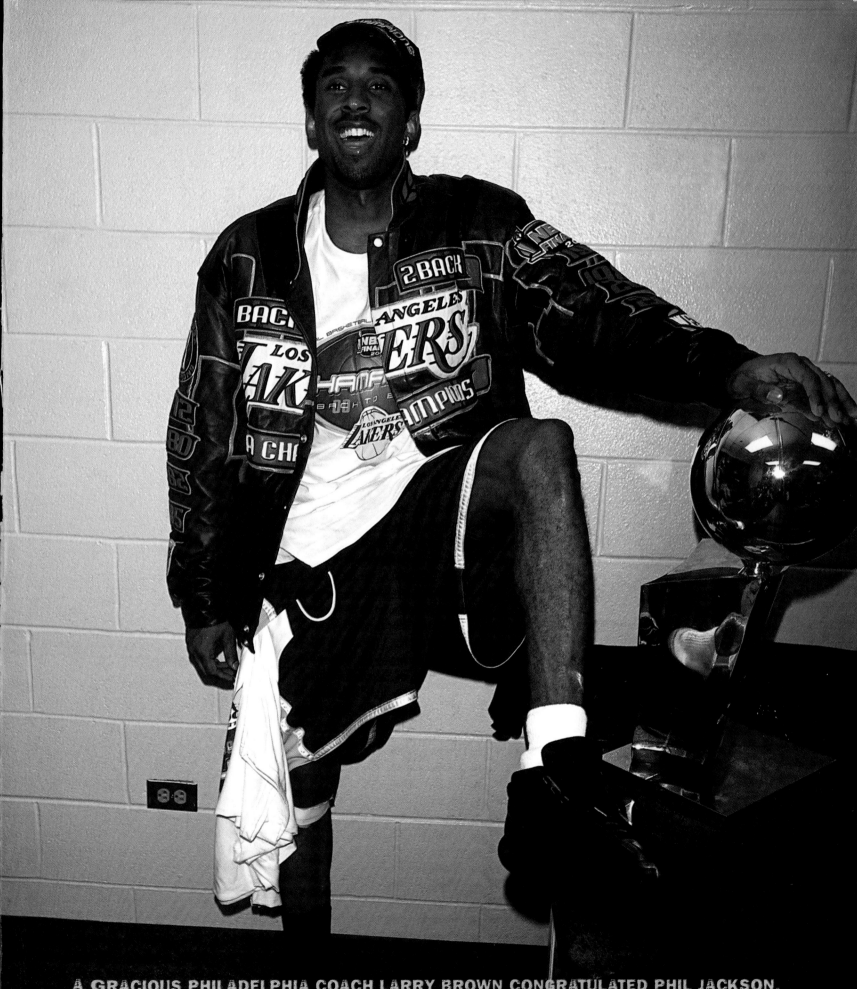

A GRACIOUS PHILADELPHIA COACH LARRY BROWN CONGRATULATED PHIL JACKSON,
WHO WON HIS EIGHTH TITLE (OPPOSITE PAGE). O'NEAL AND BRYANT THEN
CELEBRATED THE SPOILS OF VICTORY. "IT WAS AN UNBELIEVABLE RUN FOR US IN THE
PLAYOFFS," JACKSON SAID. "WE PLAYED AT A LEVEL IN WHICH WE THOUGHT AND
VISUALIZED OURSELVES PLAYING DURING THE COURSE OF THE YEAR."